THE **SIETE TABLE**

THE **SIETE TABLE**

NOURISHING MEXICAN-AMERICAN RECIPES FROM OUR KITCHEN

THE **GARZA FAMILY**
Founders of Siete Foods

With Rachel Holtzman, Bayley Wiltshire, and Rebecca Martinez
Photography by Kristin Teig and Aaron Pinkston

Recipe Development by Scarleth Aguilar, Dan Salivar,
Andrés Figueroa, Paola Briseño González, and Jeanelle Olson

HARPER WAVE
An Imprint of HarperCollins*Publishers*

HarperCollins books may be purchased for educational, business, or sales promotional use. For information, please email the Special Markets Department at SPsales@harpercollins.com.

FIRST EDITION

DESIGNED BY LEAH CARLSON-STANISIC

ALL BACKGROUND PATTERNS AND DECORATIVE BORDERS BY SHUTTERSTOCK, INC.

Library of Congress Cataloging-in-Publication Data has been applied for.

ISBN 978-0-06-321916-8

22 23 24 25 26 LSC 10 9 8 7 6 5 4 3 2 1

To our Grandma Alicia, who remains an
inspiration for everything we create—from a loving family
to homemade tortillas, Siete Family Foods,
and now this cookbook.

CONTENTS

Introduction: Gathering and Community 1

The Siete Pantry 7

1 BREAKFAST/DESAYUNO 17

2 LUNCH/ALMUERZO 41

3 SNACKS/BOTANAS 79

4 DINNER/CENA 93

5 SIDES/GUARNICIÓNES 129

6 DESSERTS/POSTRES 151

7 DRINKS/BEBIDAS 177

8 CONDIMENTS/CONDIMENTOS 197

9 OPTIONS/OPCIONES 217

10 MENUS FOR GATHERING/REUNIONES 225

Acknowledgments 261

Index 265

THE **SIETE TABLE**

THE GARZA FAMILY

ALICIA CAMPOS, GRANDMA AND AIDA'S MOTHER

"I don't use measurements, just a little bit of this and a little bit of that!"

Lover of books, number one supporter of each grandchild, expert flour tortilla maker, and inventor of the infamous cheese sauce. Loved her family like no one's business, and therefore inspired "family first, family second, business third." Officially approved Veronica's first almond flour tortilla and gave our family the only endorsement we needed to share our foods with others.

AIDA GARZA, MOM

"I always say that my mom's secret ingredient to everything she made was love. When I'm cooking, I always remember that the most important ingredient in every dish I make is love!"

The heart of our Garza and Siete family, Aida never misses an opportunity to hand out hugs in the morning to all. She's a true pioneer in the kitchen, taking after our Grandma Campos. She loves '90s rom-coms, but not as much as she loves family. Fun fact: She met our dad at the University of Texas at Austin on Speedway.

BOBBY GARZA, DAD

"I always thought we'd work together as a family, but I never imagined it would be making tortillas."

Loves yard work, exercise, and eating milanesa. Proud grandfather of ten. Eats every lunch with our beautiful mother, Aida. On Fridays after five, you might find him with a cold Bud Light in hand. Fun fact: He has eleven siblings.

LINDA GARZA, ELDEST SISTER

"I like to think that in the kitchen, I can always make something out of nothing— just like my grandma. The smells from my grandma's kitchen called everyone's attention. This is why when I'm cooking, one of the best compliments I can get is when someone walks into the kitchen and says, 'It smells delicious!'"

Oldest child and, outside of Siete, the boss of all the Garza siblings! Loves to cook, cycle, and create extravagant charcuterie boards for friends and family, and always keeps up with the latest news. Fun fact: Linda was the lead singer in the University of Texas mariachi band.

ROBERTO "ROB" GARZA, BROTHER

"Creating things together is really natural for our family. We grew up doing almost everything together. We even opened a gym as a family prior to the start of Siete. It's not a conscious thing we do—it's just our way of life."

Rob is a researcher and pun creator extraordinaire, two qualities that are only the tip of the iceberg when it comes to his many talents, which include roller skating, doing handstand push-ups on rings, and an aptitude for singing in the rain. Rob is especially considerate of others and distributes handwritten letters to the whole Siete team around Christmas each year. Fun fact: Rob has double vision.

VERONICA "VERO" GARZA, SISTER

"My mom carried my grandma's cooking refrain into her kitchen—'just a little bit of this, and a little bit of that.' Today, this is my approach to cooking and creating recipes as well. My grandma's cooking is definitely the gold standard, but I'd like to think I've gotten pretty close to re-creating many of her recipes!"

Middle child, humble mastermind, and culinary problem-solver. Our sister Veronica created our first grain-free almond flour tortilla, the product that started it all! Outside of preparing great food and snacks, Vero has a knack for interior design and can make just about any room look effortlessly charming. Fun fact: She used to be the lead singer in a band.

REBECCA "BECKY" GARZA, SISTER

"Everyone who knows me can confirm that Christmas is my favorite time of year, hands down. The lights, the tree, the joy (and of course the nutcrackers!) make me so happy, but the best part is that I get to gather with my family."

Possibly the only thing bigger than her very impressive nutcracker collection is Becky's love of family and her caring heart. Anytime we watch a sentimental movie, Becky and Aida are the first to cry. (And we love that about them!) Becky couldn't hurt a fly, but don't underestimate her strength—she'll out-lift just about anyone in the gym! Fun fact: She was valedictorian of her high school graduating class.

MIGUEL "MIKE" GARZA, BABY BROTHER

"Besides the obvious reasons to love food, it also provides a great excuse to gather together, and that's what I love most about it."

Big "little brother" vibes. Mike loves to play pranks—"Siete Scares," as we call them—but few of us have successfully scared him back. He leads with passion, encouraging everyone the same way he encouraged Vero to share her delicious tortillas with others years ago. Fun fact: He cries at every episode of *This Is Us*.

OUR STORY

As a third-generation Mexican-American family from South Texas, we grew up celebrating moments, big and small, by enjoying delicious meals. So it's safe to say that some of our favorite moments—and most moments in general—involve food. Our family of seven ate breakfast and dinner together just about every day. We have fond memories of assembling quesadillas on school nights just before *Friends* came on TV; going out to our favorite restaurants in Laredo to order pirata tacos, and chips and salsa; and inviting the neighborhood over for summertime carne asadas in the backyard.

But in 1999, our sister Veronica ("Vero," as we call her), a teenager at the time, was diagnosed with several autoimmune conditions. After researching the effects that nutrition could have on these conditions, Roberto (Rob) suggested that she try removing grains from her diet. And because our family motto is "Juntos es Mejor" (together is better), the rest of our family decided to give the grain-free lifestyle a try. To all of our amazement, we felt better. Vero's symptoms started to diminish, and we all had more energy, better digestion, and a general feeling of wellness. So, we started experimenting with swapping out other foods and ingredients that sometimes lead to undesired side effects for us, such as dairy. Sure enough, it changed our lives.

While this commitment to our health was gratifying, it wasn't always easy. It meant having to say "no" to foods that we grew up eating or had been a part of our heritage for generations. We substituted lettuce leaves for corn and flour tortillas to make tacos and avoided many other foods we love, like tortilla chips, enchiladas, and tostadas. Not only was it inconvenient and isolating, but we also felt disconnected from our heritage. So Vero began experimenting in the kitchen with alternative ingredients, trying to find a way for us to enjoy traditional foods without sacrificing any of the flavor or sentimentality.

One night, after many failed attempts to create a tortilla that tasted as good as those we grew up eating hot off the comal, Vero quietly placed her latest batch on the table without any indication that she'd made them. As each of us helped ourselves to the stack, we were amazed by how good they were—perfectly soft and chewy. Then came the real test: Grandma Campos. Our mom, Aida, brought her a batch to try. When Grandma said that Vero's almond flour tortillas tasted better than her own revered recipe for flour tortillas, we realized we had something special. In 2014, our company was born. And what better to call it than Siete Family Foods, after the seven of us.

Now, eight years after the start of Siete, we believe in the power of food more than ever. What started with our immediate family has grown into a vibrant extended familia of people who share our values of high-quality ingredients and meals made with love. We remember the days when we were hand-pressing hundreds of tortillas into the early hours of the morning, which we would then load into our cars and drive around Austin. We'd visit every grocery store in the area, giving our best sales pitches and sharing samples with buyers.

After a modest debut at our beloved Austin co-op grocer, Wheatsville, demand caught on for our packaged tortillas. As more and more people invited Siete into their kitchens, retailers took note. Eventually, we made it onto the shelves at stores across the country like Whole Foods, H-E-B, Kroger, Target, Sprouts, Costco, and Walmart. The humbling and incredible response to our products made it clear that there are people looking for grain-, gluten-, and dairy-free alternatives to their favorite foods, and the ability to enjoy some of life's most delicious rituals.

The enthusiasm we've seen for our products and the joy we aspire to bring to families is why we decided to write this book. We wanted to share our favorite recipes with everyone who is eager to enjoy delicious Mexican-American food made in the spirit of more, not less. These dishes follow the identical philosophy that we have for each of our Siete products: *salud y sabor*. It means "health and flavor"; in other words, we create flavorful foods you can enjoy whether you have dietary restrictions or simply choose to forgo grains, gluten, dairy, processed sugar,

or animal proteins. Our goal with this book is to give you delicious recipes for heritage-inspired foods—made with whole, nourishing ingredients.

One of the best compliments we receive is when people tell us that our food reminds them of their mother's/father's/aunt's/uncle's/grandma's/grandpa's cooking. Just like our Grandma Campos's stamp of approval on Vero's first grain-free tortilla was the ultimate blessing, we want all our recipes to be abuela-approved because it means that we've managed to not just nail it in the flavor department, but also evoke the kind of emotion you experience when eating a dish that feels like home, or like your childhood—like the first lick of a paleta on a hot summer day. Because food is powerful and transportive like that.

What we've found is that the magic lies not in following the most traditional recipes to the letter, but by capturing their essence. It doesn't matter if a dish no longer has dairy or grains, so long as it's deeply satisfying. It's still going to hit the spot and light up those same bits of the brain where your memories live. In order to do that, we've pulled together recipes inspired by our all-time favorite dishes, from childhood hits like flautas suaves, apple empanadas, and churros; to South Texas staples like arroz con pollo, migas, and pozole; to newer classics with an updated twist, such as tacos de coliflor and

Mexican chopped salad. And of course, no book about Mexican-American cooking would be complete without the salsas, condiments, aguas frescas, and all the other touches that make up a meal. The beauty of these recipes, like the products we offer, is that their flavor comes from simplicity. No cumbersome shopping lists and no overly complicated techniques. That's because these are dishes that come directly from our family's kitchen. They are meant to be cooked in real life.

In addition to delivering delicious recipes with a heaping side of nostalgia, we also want our food to reflect the junction between our Mexican and American heritage—or what we call "the hyphen." The hyphen represents a feeling of being situated on both sides as well as in the middle of two cultures. It's the blending of Mexican *and* American into a unique identity that we identify with more than either culture on its own. It's packing up bean tacos for a road trip instead of PB&Js, listening to George Strait while eating fajita tacos con frijoles at backyard carne asadas, waiting for the raspa truck rather than the ice cream man, understanding Spanish and speaking English, going to Taco Palenque more than Taco Bell, performing in the mariachi band and then changing into a cheerleading uniform for the football game the same night, drinking agua fresca by the pitcher, listening to Selena and the Beatles,

salsa bars and salad bars, s'mores and fresas con crema.

We wholeheartedly embrace our hyphen because it allows us to express our authenticity, which is reflected in everything we do—our food included. You'll find recipes for chilaquiles and grain-free pancakes, shrimp tostadas and shrimp cocktails, empanadas and spaghetti verde. And we can't wait to introduce you to Mexican sushi (sushi made from avocado, cream cheese, and spicy chips). All of these dishes perfectly sum up our family's culture, which is not defined by just one influence, whether it's our customs, our geography, our food, or our health. We believe in putting the pieces together in a way that feels right for you. That's also why we've included a number of substitutions throughout this book, such as our corn-free masa and vegan chorizo. We want you to tweak these recipes to suit your needs and tastes. And if you want to wrap up that taco or burrito in a corn or flour tortilla? That's fine by us too!

More than anything, though, this book is written in the spirit of gathering and community—because food is a powerful vehicle for these values. Our goal is for these recipes to inspire you to share delicious meals with neighbors, friends, and family, which is why we've also included five curated menus to give you the blueprint you need to confidently fill all the seats at your table. In addition to being balanced, we like to think that the best quality of these recipes is that they are as inclusive as they are tasty. Because they are suited for a wide range of dietary needs and preferences, there's no crowd that they can't satisfy. We also hope that you can set aside any trepidation you might feel about cooking for a crowd (even if it's just your family) and remember that there is nothing that a big plate of fresh tortillas—and a round of Mexican martinis—can't fix.

We hope these recipes encourage you to embrace ingredients and techniques that you may not have tried before—or new ideas about dishes that you have had, but are different than ours—and then share those experiences with loved ones. These recipes exist because of their place in our culture. They've continued to headline our family's menus because they're undeniably delicious, but they are also memories in and of themselves. We offer the meals in this book as a way to honor the ones we love and the ones who have come before us. May they inspire new traditions that send your heart fluttering and your stomach grumbling with anticipation—traditions that your loved ones will cherish, like the fresh pot of beans and tortillas awaiting us each time we visited our Grandma Campos. Or waking up to the smell of the café con leche that our parents brewed and enjoyed before the sun rose every single morning.

Here's to new memories in your kitchen and at your table. We're glad you're here and we hope you're hungry!

Juntos es Mejor,
The Garzas, Your Siete Family

Siete was born when Veronica experimented with innovative ingredients to create more options for our family to enjoy the foods we love without sacrificing our health. When it comes to eating, our philosophy is *salud y sabor*—health and flavor. That said, it's important to us that our recipes are inclusive. We believe in having options that allow anyone to bake, cook, and enjoy their favorite foods in ways that are right for them and their health goals. That's why we've included a number of substitutions throughout this book.

Since some of the ingredients we use throughout these recipes might be new to you, we wanted to take a minute to properly introduce some of our go-to staples.

ADOBO: Adobo sauce is an earthy red marinade made from chipotle chiles and spices like garlic, paprika, oregano, salt, and vinegar. We enjoy its smoky flavor on chicken, pork, and chiles.

ALMOND FLOUR: Almond flour is a course, dense flour, and it was one of the first ingredients that Veronica experimented with in the kitchen. In fact, almonds inspired our first company name, Must B Nutty, since our first product was an almond flour tortilla. These days, we love using almond flour for all our baking needs because of how well it binds a recipe, especially in tortillas, cookies, empanadas, and conchas.

ANCHO CHILES: These are large, mild, dried poblano peppers. They taste sweet and chocolatey, and they are often used in Mexican soups, sauces, and marinades.

APPLE CIDER VINEGAR: A little acidity and tang is just the thing to make the flavor of a dish really come to life. Apple cider vinegar—next to lime juice—is one of our favorite clean ways to amp up flavor profiles, especially in hot sauce, enchilada sauce, and salsas.

AVOCADO OIL: We avoid picking favorites, but there's no denying that our family loves avocado oil. Avocados are a popular crop in Mexico, and we love avocado oil for its neutral taste and high smoke point (meaning that it is more resistant to heat and doesn't burn as quickly). In fact, we always have avocado oil on hand for frying tortilla chips, kettle-cooking potato chips, or thickening our favorite salsas and dips.

CASHEW CREMA: Crema is a thick, rich, and creamy condiment that's used to add tangy brightness to dishes such as enchiladas, soup, and tacos, and it can also help dial down the heat. Because our family is dairy-free, we make our crema from cashews. We know making crema from nuts might sound a little crazy, and it is—crazy good.

CASSAVA: Also known as manioc, tapioca, and yuca, cassava is a root vegetable and staple crop in many parts of the world, including Latin America, Africa, and Asia. Cassava flour has a fine texture and a neutral flavor, which makes it a versatile substitute flour. We particularly love using cassava flour because it yields tortillas that are soft, tasty, and gluten-, grain-, and nut-free.

CHICHARRONES: *Chicharrones* is the Spanish word for "pork rinds" that are fried until they puff up. They smell and taste a bit like bacon but resemble a chip or cracker and are usually enjoyed as a crunchy, salty, and satisfying snack (we like them with hot sauce!). In a meal, they can be simmered in salsa or cooked into scrambled eggs.

CHIPOTLE CHILES: Chipotle chiles are essentially jalapeños that have been ripened until they are red, then smoked and dried. As a result, they have a similar heat level to jalapeños but are distinctly smoky in aroma and flavor. Chipotles are often used as a seasoning, but they are also added to salsas, *caldos* (flavorful broths), and adobo sauce.

COCONUT AMINOS: Coconut aminos deliver a similar flavor yet slightly sweeter profile than soy sauce, while also being soy-free, gluten-free, and vegan. There are few ingredients that pack the same unique, salty savoriness as coconut aminos—which is why we use it in marinades and condiments.

COCONUT OIL: Use this versatile oil by the spoonful to add a rich flavor to your sautéed, cooked, and baked creations.

COCONUT SUGAR: There's no denying that our family has a sweet tooth. So whenever the craving for buñuelos, churros, or cookies hits, we reach for the coconut sugar, which brings a subtle caramelized flavor to baked goods.

GHEE: Oh em ghee . . . can you believe it's clarified, unsalted butter? "Clarified" means that the milk solids, lactose, and casein have been removed. This rich, creamy fat makes for a versatile butter substitute for those with allergies to lactose and casein.

GUAJILLO CHILES: These are mild chiles that are widely popular in Mexican dishes, cooking, and culture. They are most often used dried and added to caldos, sauces, marinades, moles, and, of course, salsas!

HABANERO CHILES: Depending on your heat tolerance and how they're prepared, these super-spicy chiles will either leave you pleasantly feeling the heat or quickly reaching for the closest glass of agua fresca. Our family likes to put flavor before fire, so if we call for using habaneros in our recipes, we usually tame their heat by removing the seeds so that the chiles don't overpower the meal.

JALAPEÑO CHILES: Jalapeños are used very commonly as a flavoring element—as well as a pickled topping or garnish—for just about any dish in Mexican cooking. These chiles are spicy, but they are by no means the spiciest chile. Jalapeños infuse a pleasant heat that adds a kick of flavor to tacos, tostadas, guacamole, salsa, and many other classic dishes.

JAMAICA (HIBISCUS FLOWERS): These flowers are as beautiful to look at as they are delicious to drink when steeped in tea or aguas frescas. They have a tart, tangy flavor and a beautiful deep red color.

LIME: Acidity and tartness are two flavors that we come back to, lime after lime. A squeeze of this citrus fruit is the perfect way to finish off a fish taco, add a little zest to papitas, jazz up a cold drink—the list goes on!

MAPLE SYRUP: We're not strict on sweeteners—when it comes to sweet, we say, you do you. We'll simply offer that, over the years, we've come to love maple syrup for both its natural sweetness and cooking versatility.

MEXICAN OREGANO: This herb is not the same as the familiar Mediterranean-derived oregano of the mint family, which is common in Italian and Greek cooking. Mexican oregano is more aromatic and has a peppery flavor. It lends notes of citrus and a bit of licorice to dishes like soups, sauces, and stews.

PILONCILLO: Also known as Mexican brown sugar, *piloncillo* is a raw form of pure cane sugar that is not processed and has a natural brown color. Its flavor has a complex richness similar to molasses. It is often cone-shaped, and you simply remove what you need to sweeten drinks like café de olla, or to deepen the flavor of sauces.

POBLANO CHILES: Poblanos have a fresh "green" taste that's similar to green bell peppers but with a little more heat. These chiles have many uses, which range from chiles rellenos (essentially Mexican stuffed peppers), caldos, rice, sauce, and spaghetti verde.

SERRANO CHILES: These are similar in appearance to jalapeños, but smaller and a whole lot spicier. We use serranos in salsas, sauces, guacamole, and as a topping for many dishes. Though this chile's got a hot kick, it is a staple, and when used sparingly, it can add flavor and depth to just about any dish.

TAMARIND: This is a fruit that grows as a pod in trees, and the sweet, tangy pulp is perfect in iced tea or paletas, or as the base of our favorite sweet, spicy, sour candies. It's a nostalgic flavor that takes us back to our childhood in Laredo.

CASHEWS

COCONUT SUGAR

HIBISCUS

ALMOND FLOUR

PILONCILLO

MEXICAN OREGANO

CASSAVA FLOUR

CINNAMON

TAMARIND

JALAPEÑO

HABANERO

CHILE DE ARBOL

POBLANO

SERRANO

GUAJILLO

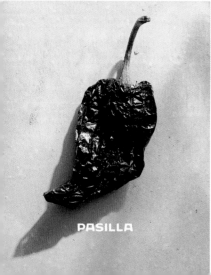

PASILLA

ANCHO

A NOTE ON CHILES

You'll notice that a number of our recipes include fresh and dried chiles, namely because they're one of the most flavorful ingredients that you can add to a dish. While we call for removing their seeds, you're welcome to leave them in for an even more intense dose of heat if, like us, that's something you enjoy!

AN INTRODUCTION TO OUR TORTILLAS

We're proud of all the love and hard work that was poured into every single one of our Siete products, and we are always excited to share them with people. But we would never want you to feel like you could only make these recipes if you went out and bought our products. That's why, in any instance where we call for an item we make—whether it's a tortilla, chip, sauce, or seasoning—we'll always give you the option to use whatever product is most convenient for or desirable to you. That said, should you decide to experiment with our tortillas, we wanted to offer some guidance.

PRODUCT	FLAVOR	WHY AND HOW THEY'RE GREAT
ALMOND FLOUR TORTILLAS	Buttery, savory, and fluffy and thick like a flour tortilla.	These are equally delicious with sweet or savory toppings. The natural oils from the almonds mean no extra oil is needed to make tostadas, Mexican pizzas, crunchy "croutons," soup strips, or homemade tortilla chips.
CASSAVA FLOUR TORTILLAS	Starchy, light, and plain, like a mix between a corn and flour tortilla.	These cassava and coconut flour tortillas are a staple for tacos, wraps, and enchiladas. Their starchy, pliable texture and versatile flavor is great with toppings of any kind. They can also be baked into a recipe, and then frozen and saved for later.
CHICKPEA FLOUR TORTILLAS	When heated, has a soft and supple texture like a corn tortilla. Has a mildly earthy taste of legumes and olive oil.	Our chickpea flour tortillas char beautifully when heated over flames. They're also extremely pliable, which makes them great for recipes that call for wrapping and folding, such as tacos, burritos, crepes, and wraps. Their flavor makes them well suited for savory fillings.

1

BREAKFAST/DESAYUNO

The smell of refried beans and fresh tortillas from our Grandma Campos's kitchen comes to mind when we hear the word "breakfast." We also think of warm café con leche and sizzling bacon, and sitting down to the large feast of foods our mom had been in the kitchen preparing while we slept in on Sundays. To our family, breakfast is about more than food. It's tradition.

On Saturdays throughout our childhood, our family could be found jostling one another around the table, helping ourselves to a huge buffet of food made by our mother, Aida. Our plates would be stacked with traditional Mexican and American dishes like pancakes, bacon, beans, potatoes, and all kinds of egg dishes, like huevos con papas and migas. Other mornings, the kitchen would be buzzing with rushed activity as each of us took turns to quickly heat up tortillas over the comal or cast-iron skillet, using them to scarf down leftover beans before rushing out of the house to school, work, or the next scheduled activity. Sometimes our dad would bring home breakfast tacos from our favorite restaurants in Laredo—along with plenty of extra little containers of salsas and pico, which were often saved and baked into breakfasts like huevos a la mexicana in the following days.

On the occasion that we went out for breakfast as a family, we'd choose from Mexican classics like mariachi tacos and breakfast plates like barbacoa and chorizo con huevo, or, of course, American breakfast staples like bacon and maybe a side of pancakes with syrup. Though, even when we went this route, we'd still order beans and tortillas for the table. And given our deep love for breakfast, perhaps it's no surprise that we also loved having breakfast for dinner—a tradition we encourage you to try out with these recipes.

MIGAS

SERVES 4 | 35 MINUTES | GF, DF

Growing up in a household of seven (Siete!), there have always been certain considerations around food, even before we went grain-free. To name a few, serving foods that would please the palates of five kids with different preferences, being resourceful by making meals from ingredients that were already on hand, and preparing dishes that go a long way. Migas was in frequent rotation because it checked all of these boxes. Perfect for putting day-old tortillas to use, this simple dish calls for little more than what you already have in your fridge and pantry—tortilla scraps, eggs, and onions. You can also dress it up or down, depending on who's at the table. Our dad, Bobby, prefers migas with just the eggs and onions, while our eldest sister, Linda, likes to spice up hers with tomatoes and chiles.

4 Siete Grain Free Almond Flour Tortillas, or tortillas of your choice

¼ cup plus 1 teaspoon avocado oil

1½ teaspoons sea salt, plus more to taste

6 large eggs

Freshly ground black pepper

1 large tomato, diced

1 jalapeño, stemmed, seeded, and finely chopped

1 avocado, sliced

Your favorite hot sauce, for serving

Refried Beans (page 131), or store-bought, warmed, for serving (optional)

1 Cut the tortillas into ¾-inch squares.

2 In a large nonstick skillet over medium-high heat, heat 2 tablespoons of the oil. Add half of the tortilla squares and cook, stirring and tossing, until they are golden and crispy, 5 to 7 minutes. Immediately transfer the crispy tortilla squares to a large bowl and toss them with ½ teaspoon of the salt, or more to taste. Transfer the tortilla squares once again to a paper towel–lined plate to drain. Repeat with 2 more tablespoons of the oil and the remaining tortillas.

3 In a medium bowl, whisk the eggs with ½ teaspoon of the remaining salt and pepper to taste until well combined. Set aside.

continued

4 In the same skillet over medium heat, combine the tomato and jalapeño. Cook until the tomatoes have released some of their juices, about 4 minutes. Add the remaining 1 teaspoon of oil to the skillet and reduce the heat to low. Add the eggs, using a spatula to gently fold and combine them with the vegetables. Cook until curds start to set but the mixture is still moist, 2 to 3 minutes.

5 Add the salted tortilla squares and gently fold them in to incorporate. Cook just enough to keep the tortilla squares crisp, about 3 more minutes. Season with salt and pepper.

6 Garnish the migas with the sliced avocado and hot sauce. Serve with a side of refried beans, if desired.

MARIACHIS

SERVES 4 | 40 MINUTES | GF

Our mom likes to tell this story of the first time she heard her father-in-law, our grandpa, mention that he was getting "mariachis" for breakfast: *Mariachis . . . for breakfast?* She couldn't understand why he'd round up a traditional Mexican folk band in the early hours of the morning. When he showed up with a bag full of breakfast tacos, that's when she learned that "mariachis" is a common name for breakfast tacos in Laredo. These tacos are filled with a variety of proteins, salsas, and toppings, but one of our favorites is stuffed with potatoes and eggs, and topped with roasted tomato salsa.

½ pound Yukon Gold or red potatoes, cut into ½-inch cubes

1½ teaspoons sea salt

2 tablespoons avocado oil

½ medium yellow onion, finely diced

½ teaspoon stemmed, seeded, and finely minced serrano chile

¼ teaspoon freshly ground black pepper

8 large eggs

½ cup shredded mozzarella or cheddar cheese

4 Siete Grain Free Almond Flour Tortillas, or tortillas of your choice

Salsa Tatemada (page 201), for serving

1 In a small saucepan, cover the potatoes with 1 inch of water. Over medium-high heat, bring the water to a boil and season with 1 teaspoon of the salt. Reduce the heat to medium and cook at a rapid simmer until the potatoes are easily pierced with a paring knife but still firm, about 7 minutes. Drain the potatoes in a colander.

2 In a large nonstick skillet over medium heat, heat 1 tablespoon of the oil. Add the drained potatoes, cooking briefly until the potatoes start to get golden and crispy, about 4 minutes. Add the onions, serrano, ¼ teaspoon of the remaining salt, and the pepper. Cook, stirring frequently, until the onions are translucent and the potatoes are crispy, 4 to 6 minutes. Remove the pan from the heat and transfer the mixture to a small bowl.

continued

3 In a medium bowl, whisk the eggs with the remaining ¼ teaspoon salt until uniform.

4 Set the same nonstick skillet over low heat and add the remaining 1 tablespoon oil. Add the eggs and cook, using a spatula to push and fold the eggs from the edges toward the center. Continue folding with the spatula occasionally until large, fluffy curds form, 5 to 7 minutes. Sprinkle the cheese over the eggs and gently fold it in. Remove the pan from the heat and set aside.

5 Heat a large sauté pan or a cast-iron skillet over medium-high heat. Warm each tortilla for 5 to 10 seconds per side, flipping once or twice. Transfer the warmed tortillas to a foil packet or clean kitchen towel to cover and keep warm. Repeat with the remaining tortillas.

6 To serve, spoon about ½ cup of the egg scramble and ¼ cup of the potato mixture onto each tortilla and fold it over. Serve immediately with the salsa tatemada.

CHOCOLATE AND VANILLA CONCHAS

MAKES 8 CONCHAS | 2 HOURS 15 MINUTES | GF, DF, V [OPTION]

Conchas were a treat our mom enjoyed during her summers in Mexico as a young girl. Her tía would wake up before her and the rest of her cousins, head over to the panadería, and fill up a basket with *pan dulces* (sweet breads), including conchas. We're happy to share this gluten-free version all these years later, so you too can know the joy of conchas toasted, sliced, and smeared with some butter. Enjoy these with a cup of cafecito in the morning, or for *merienda*, as a sweet afternoon snack.

NOTE: The flour used to make these conchas results in a denser pastry than those made with eggs and all-purpose flour.

FOR THE CONCHAS

1 cup oat milk or dairy-free milk of your choice

1 teaspoon active dry yeast

2 cups white rice flour, plus more for dusting

1 cup potato starch

¼ cup coconut flour

¼ cup coconut sugar

½ teaspoon psyllium husk powder

½ teaspoon sea salt

¼ cup melted coconut oil, cooled

FOR THE CHOCOLATE AND VANILLA TOPPING

1½ cups powdered sugar, plus more for dusting

¾ cup coconut shortening

3 tablespoons white rice flour

¼ teaspoon ground cinnamon

Pinch of sea salt

1 teaspoon vanilla extract

2 teaspoons cocoa powder

1 Make the concha dough: In a small bowl, add the milk and yeast with 1 cup of lukewarm water. Mix to combine and let the mixture sit until the yeast activates and bubbles are visible on the surface, about 10 minutes.

2 In a medium bowl, combine the rice flour, potato starch, coconut flour, coconut sugar, psyllium husk powder, and salt.

3 In a stand mixer fitted with the paddle attachment, combine the yeast mixture and melted oil on medium speed. Add the flour mixture and mix

continued

until well combined. The dough will be very soft, like a thick cookie batter.

4 Preheat the oven to 400°F. Line a baking sheet with parchment paper and set aside.

5 Divide the dough into 8 equal pieces. Dust your hands with rice flour and shape each piece into a small puck. Arrange the formed dough pieces on the prepared baking sheet and lightly cover them with plastic wrap. Let the dough sit in a warm place for 1 hour or overnight in the refrigerator. If refrigerating, you'll need to take the dough out of the refrigerator 30 minutes before baking.

6 **Make the topping:** In a small bowl, combine the powdered sugar, shortening, rice flour, cinnamon, salt, and vanilla. Transfer half of the mixture to another small bowl. Add the cocoa powder to one of the bowls and combine well.

7 Divide each topping into 8 equal pieces. Take 1 piece of the vanilla topping with 1 piece of the chocolate topping and form into a ball. Use powdered sugar to dust your hands and roll the colors together. Repeat with the remaining pieces of the topping.

8 Using your hands or a rolling pin, flatten each ball so that it's large enough to cover the top surface of each piece of concha dough. Place a piece of topping on top of each concha and lightly press them together. If you have a concha cutter, lightly dust it with powdered sugar and press down on each concha to make the "seashell" mark. You can make a similar design by making 4 to 5 3-inch slits in the topping with a paring knife.

9 Bake the conchas for 14 minutes, until golden brown and fragrant. After baking, let the conchas sit at room temperature until they have completely cooled to allow the topping to harden and to get the best texture on the inside. (The conchas can get gummy if they're sliced while still hot.) These are best enjoyed the day they are made.

BARBACOA

SERVES 6 TO 8 | 3 HOURS 30 MINUTES | GF, DF

Barbacoa was a Sunday morning tradition in our house. It is a typical South Texas breakfast, especially with all the great taco places in Laredo. Unlike the often heavily seasoned barbacoa that's typically served at lunch or dinner, this version is made with a short list of ingredients and served with a large pile of tortillas for tacos. When Vero makes this simple version—which is now our mom's favorite—she adds only salt, pepper, garlic, and onion before slow-cooking the meat to perfection. All you need to add are tortillas, limes, salsa, and a freshly poured cup of coffee.

NOTE: Barbacoa, traditionally made with the entire beef head, is now often made from beef tongue, beef cheeks, or a combination of the two. Braising meat with high fat content is essential for this dish, which is why we suggest using beef cheeks or adding oxtail to your roast for this recipe.

½ large yellow onion, roughly chopped

¼ cup apple cider vinegar

4 garlic cloves, peeled and left whole

2 teaspoons dried Mexican oregano leaves

2 whole black peppercorns

2 teaspoons sea salt, plus more to taste

4 pounds beef cheeks, or 3 pounds beef chuck roast plus 1½ pounds oxtail

Freshly ground black pepper

1 dried bay leaf

8 Siete Grain Free Cassava Flour Tortillas, or tortillas of your choice, warmed

Lime wedges, for serving

Salsa Tatemada (page 201), for serving

1 Position a rack in the middle of the oven. Preheat the oven to 325°F.

2 In a high-speed blender, combine the onion, vinegar, garlic, oregano, and peppercorns, plus 1 cup of water and 1 teaspoon of the salt, and blend until completely smooth. Set aside.

3 In a Dutch oven or large baking dish, add the meat and season with the remaining 1 teaspoon of salt and pepper to taste. Pour the onion and spice puree over the meat, add the bay leaf, and cover tightly with a lid or foil. Place the pot on the

continued

middle rack of the oven and bake for 2 to 3 hours, checking every 30 minutes after the second hour for tenderness. If there is less than 1 cup of liquid left, add ½ cup of water before returning the meat to the oven. When the meat is very tender and easy to pull apart, remove the pot from the oven and let it rest, still covered, for 30 minutes.

4 Transfer the meat to a large bowl or platter and gently pull it apart into large chunks. Discard the bay leaf and pour some of the cooking broth over the meat. Season with salt as needed.

5 Serve the barbacoa with a stack of warm tortillas, lime wedges, and salsa tatemada.

CHILAQUILES

SERVES 4 | 25 MINUTES | GF, DF, V

We think of chilaquiles as a more "dressed up" version of migas because they call for similar ingredients but also have chicken and red or green sauce on top. There really is no right or wrong way to cook them, but we love when the crispy tortillas soak up just enough sauce to make them slightly crunchy, yet tender enough to almost melt as soon as they reach your mouth.

2 tablespoons avocado oil or your favorite oil for frying, plus more

8 Siete Grain Free Almond Flour Tortillas, or tortillas of your choice, each cut into 6 triangles

3 Roma tomatoes

3 dried guajillo chiles, stemmed and seeded

3 dried arbol chiles, stemmed and seeded

¼ white onion

3 garlic cloves

1½ teaspoons white vinegar

1½ teaspoons sea salt

Cashew Crema (page 207), for serving

Marinated Red Onions (page 213), for serving

Chile Oil (page 199), for serving

1 In a high-sided skillet over medium-high heat, heat about 1 inch of avocado oil to 350°F.

2 Working in batches, fry the tortilla pieces until golden brown, about 1 minute. Transfer the fried tortillas to a wire rack set over a baking sheet to drain.

3 In a small saucepan over medium-high heat, add the tomatoes and enough water to cover. Bring to a boil, reduce the heat to medium, and cook the tomatoes until their skins start to burst, about 5 minutes.

4 Transfer the tomatoes and 1 cup of their cooking water, plus the guajillo and arbol chiles, the onion, garlic, vinegar, and salt to a high-speed blender and blend until completely smooth.

5 In a medium skillet over medium heat, heat the 2 tablespoons avocado oil. Add the salsa and bring to a simmer. Toss in the crispy fried tortillas and cook just until all of the tortilla pieces are coated in the salsa. Divide the mixture among plates and top with crema, marinated red onions, and chile oil.

HUEVOS RANCHEROS

SERVES 4 | 30 MINUTES | GF, DF [OPTION]

Where we're from, huevos rancheros are considered a "must"—must have on the menu, must order, must try, must fall in love, must repeat. This dish starts with a warmed tortilla, which gets topped with two eggs and a tomato-based salsa. Serve it with a side of refried beans, and you'll get a taste of many of our breakfast favorites in a single dish.

FOR THE RANCHERO SAUCE

1 pound Roma tomatoes

1 serrano chile, stemmed and seeded

2 tablespoons avocado oil

1 small white onion, finely diced

3 garlic cloves, roughly chopped

1½ teaspoons sea salt

FOR THE HUEVOS RANCHEROS

1 tablespoon avocado oil

4 large eggs

Sea salt and freshly ground black pepper

1 cup Refried Beans (page 131), or store-bought, warmed

8 Siete Grain Free Almond Flour Tortillas, or tortillas of your choice, warmed

1 cup shredded Oaxaca cheese or shredded dairy-free cheese of your choice

¼ cup chopped fresh cilantro

1 avocado, sliced

Marinated Red Onions (page 213), for serving

1 Make the ranchero sauce: In a large cast-iron skillet over medium-high heat, add the tomatoes and serrano and let them char for a few minutes per side, until the tomatoes start to burst, about 5 minutes. Transfer the tomatoes and serrano, plus 1 cup of water, to a high-speed blender and blend until smooth.

2 In a small saucepan over medium heat, heat the avocado oil. Add the onions and garlic and cook, stirring frequently, until the onions are golden brown, about 5 minutes. Add the blended tomato mixture and bring the sauce to a boil. Stir in the salt, remove the pot from the heat, and cover to keep the sauce warm until ready to use.

3 Make the huevos rancheros: In a large non-stick skillet over medium-high heat, heat the oil. Crack the eggs into the pan, season with salt and pepper, and cook to your liking.

4 Spread about 2 tablespoons of the refried beans on a tortilla. Top with another tortilla, followed by another 2 tablespoons of the beans. Top

with a fried egg and spoon the ranchero sauce on and around the egg. Repeat with the remaining beans, tortillas, and eggs. Add the cheese on top and finish with the cilantro and a few slices of avocado. Serve with the marinated red onions.

HUEVOS A LA MEXICANA

SERVES 4 | 20 MINUTES | GF, DF

"A la mexicana" refers to the use of three primary ingredients—tomatoes, onions, and jalapeños—representing the colors of the Mexican flag. This delicious egg dish is just the thing when you want a quick and simple-to-make breakfast. Plus, you can improvise by adding your favorite ingredients and creating your own variations. One time-saving shortcut is using leftover pico de gallo in place of the onion, jalapeño, and tomato. You can also add chorizo, ham, or sausage to make an extra-savory version.

8 large eggs

Sea salt and freshly ground black pepper

3 tablespoons avocado or extra-virgin olive oil

1 small yellow onion, diced

1 jalapeño chile, minced

1 Roma tomato, diced

2 tablespoons chopped fresh cilantro

Salsa Roja (page 45), for serving

Lime wedges, for serving

Your favorite hot sauce, for serving

Siete Grain Free Cassava Flour Tortillas, or tortillas of your choice, warmed, for serving (optional)

1 Crack the eggs into a medium bowl, season with salt and pepper, and beat until uniform. Set aside.

2 In a large nonstick skillet over medium-high heat, heat the oil. Add the onion and jalapeño and season with salt and pepper. Cook, stirring frequently, until the onion is translucent and softened, 3 to 4 minutes. Add the tomatoes and cook, stirring frequently, until their juice has reduced slightly, 3 to 4 minutes. If the mixture looks a bit dry, add another teaspoon or two of oil and let it heat.

3 Pour in the eggs and use a spatula to scramble and turn to incorporate them with the vegetables. Cook until the eggs begin to lose their shine just slightly, then remove the pan from the heat. Stir in the cilantro and divide the egg mixture among 4 plates. Serve with the salsa, lime wedges, hot sauce, and warm tortillas, if you like.

CHICHARRONES EN SALSA

SERVES 4 | 40 MINUTES | GF, DF

Chips and salsa, carne en salsa, bistec en salsa, pollo en salsa, papas en salsa, mariscos en salsa . . . there's a pattern here, and for good reason. We love salsa! And we especially love to put different foods in salsa, including *chicharrones*, or crispy pork rinds. It's a hearty traditional breakfast that's usually served with refried beans and has a special place at our table and in our hearts.

2 pounds tomatillos, husked

2 serrano chiles, stemmed, cut in half, and seeded

3 garlic cloves, peeled and left whole

¾ cup chopped fresh cilantro

¾ teaspoon sea salt

8 ounces chicharrones (fried pork rinds)

2 cups Refried Beans (page 131), or store-bought, warmed, for serving

Siete Grain Free Cassava Flour Tortillas, or tortillas of your choice, warmed, for serving

1 In a large skillet over medium heat, add the tomatillos, serranos, and 3 cups of water. Bring to a boil and cook, stirring occasionally, until the tomatillos are soft, 10 minutes.

2 Transfer the tomatillo mixture plus 1½ cups of the cooking liquid to a blender along with the garlic, cilantro, and salt. Puree until smooth.

3 Add salsa verde back to the pan and set over medium heat. Simmer to thicken the salsa slightly, about 10 minutes. Add the chicharrones to the salsa and cook until softened, 30 seconds to 1 minute. Taste and adjust the salt as needed.

4 Serve hot with the refried beans and warm tortillas.

CRISPY PAPAS

SERVES 4 | 30 MINUTES | GF, DF, V

Growing up, our mom cooked with potatoes almost daily—scrambled with eggs for papas con huevo, rolled inside tortillas for flautas de papa, or in this case, fried with scallions and serranos as crispy papas. One day Miguel came home from school and excitedly told us that he used a deep fryer in his Home Economics class to make the crispiest chicken nuggets and papas. The very next day, she went out and bought her first air fryer! It was useful for mornings when she'd make especially large batches of crispy papas, but she still prefers the skillet method because it reminds her of special moments watching her mom make breakfast for the whole family.

1½ pounds russet potatoes, peeled and cut into 1-inch cubes

Sea salt

¼ cup avocado oil

Freshly ground black pepper

2 scallions, white and light green parts only, sliced

½ serrano chile, stemmed, seeded, and minced

2 tablespoons chopped fresh cilantro

3 tablespoons Cashew Crema (page 207)

Lime wedges, for serving

Marinated Red Onions (page 213), for serving

1 In a large pot over medium-high heat, cover the potatoes with cold water and a large pinch of salt. Bring to a boil and cook for 8 to 10 minutes, until the potatoes are tender when pierced with a fork. Drain the potatoes and set aside.

2 Heat the oil in a large cast-iron or nonstick skillet over medium-high heat. Add the potatoes, season with salt and pepper, and cook, stirring, until they begin to brown at the edges, 4 to 5 minutes. Gently toss in the scallions and serrano and cook for 30 seconds. Taste and adjust the seasoning, if needed. Sprinkle the cilantro over the top and serve with the crema, limes, and marinated onions.

GRAIN-FREE PANCAKES

Grandma Campos could do no wrong when it came to making food the whole family would enjoy. A true pioneer in the kitchen, she never measured ingredients. It was her experimental spirit that inspired us to make pancakes using almond flour when we went grain-free. Topped with a drizzle of sweet, creamy dairy-free cajeta, these pancakes are the perfect blend of Mexican heritage and American culture.

¼ cup flax meal

2 cups almond flour

1¼ cups cassava flour

½ cup tapioca flour

2 teaspoons baking soda

1 teaspoon sea salt

1 cup maple syrup

½ cup plus 1 tablespoon avocado oil

2 tablespoons vanilla extract

Coconut Cajeta (page 161),
for serving

½ cup chopped pecans, for serving

1 In a small bowl, whisk the flax meal with 1 cup of water and let sit for 5 minutes.

2 In a large bowl, whisk together the almond flour, cassava flour, tapioca flour, baking soda, and salt. Add the flax mixture, maple syrup,

½ cup of the avocado oil, the vanilla, and 1 cup of water and whisk until smooth. If the batter is too thick, add up to another ¼ cup of water to thin out.

3 In a large nonstick skillet over medium heat, heat the remaining 1 tablespoon of avocado oil. Working in batches, add the batter to the pan in about ¼-cup dollops. Cook the pancakes undisturbed for about 3 minutes on the first side, until the top of the batter is bubbling. Flip the pancakes and cook for another 1 to 2 minutes, until cooked through. Transfer the pancakes to a serving plate and repeat with the remaining batter. If desired, cover the finished pancakes with a kitchen towel or keep the plate in a low oven to keep warm as you cook the remaining pancakes.

4 Top the pancakes with the coconut cajeta and chopped pecans.

2

LUNCH/ALMUERZO

Simple, quick, and delicious—that's what lunch is all about to our family. Growing up, we'd pick up our favorite pirata tacos from Taco Palenque, order pillowy flautas suaves from restaurants around town, unwrap freshly made bean tacos our mom packed in foil that morning, or sit down to a sandwich with potato chips and hot sauce on the side.

Regular attendance at school kept us from eating lunch as a family during the week, but our parents never missed their midday meal together. It was one of those traditions that was so unwavering that we thought of it less as a "tradition" than part of the family's everyday routine. When any of us kids stayed home "sick" from school (whether we were really suffering or playing up our symptoms a bit!), we knew we would get to join our mom and dad for lunch and enjoy some special time with them. While this wasn't our *only* motivation to stay home from school, it was certainly a bonus.

Today, lunch is often consumed on the go—you can find many of us quickly slurping caldo de pollo between meetings, frying a few flautas de papa in a pan for ourselves and our kids, or ordering ceviche with chips off any menu that offers it. But no matter the dish or the location, the idea remains the same: pausing—however briefly—to enjoy tasty food that fills bellies and keeps us going throughout busy days.

TORTILLA SOUP

SERVES 3 TO 4 | 1 HOUR 45 MINUTES | GF, DF

When the weather dips below 70 degrees—which is considered "chilly" in South Texas—everyone makes soup. Tortilla soup is a family favorite because it incorporates a richly flavored caldo de pollo broth along with a hearty heap of braised chicken thighs, topped by delicious accompaniments like tortilla strips, avocado, radishes, and fresh cilantro.

FOR THE SOUP

1 pound (4 or 5) Roma tomatoes, halved

1 small yellow onion, quartered

2 garlic cloves, peeled and left whole

3 dried guajillo chiles, stemmed and seeded

1 teaspoon sea salt, plus more to taste

1½ pounds boneless, skinless chicken thighs

2 tablespoons extra-virgin olive oil

7 cups chicken or vegetable broth

6 sprigs of fresh cilantro, knotted together or tied with kitchen twine

Avocado oil, or your favorite oil, for frying

8 Siete Grain Free Almond Flour Tortillas, or tortillas of your choice, cut into ½-inch strips

FOR SERVING

2 avocados, diced

1 cup chopped fresh cilantro

6 radishes, thinly sliced

Lime wedges

1 Make the soup: Place the tomatoes (cut side-up), onions, and garlic cloves in a cold cast-iron skillet. Set the skillet over medium-high heat and let the vegetables toast for about 5 minutes, until lightly charred. Flip and continue charring for another 3 minutes. Add the guajillos and toast for about 1 minute on each side, until they become slightly soft and pliable. Transfer the tomatoes, onions, garlic, and guajillos to a medium saucepan and cover with water. Place the saucepan over medium-high heat and bring to a boil. Reduce the heat to medium and simmer for 12 to 15 minutes, until the tomatoes have cooked down and the mixture is slightly thickened.

2 Transfer the tomatoes, onion, garlic, guajillos, about 1 cup of the simmering liquid, and the salt to a high-speed blender and blend until completely smooth. Set aside.

3 Season the chicken thighs generously with salt and set aside.

continued

4 Heat the olive oil in a large, heavy-bottomed pot over medium-high heat. Add the tomato and chile mixture and cook, stirring frequently, for 10 to 12 minutes, until thickened and darkened in color. Add the chicken thighs, turning once to coat them completely in the tomato and chile mixture. Add about 1 cup of the broth, cover, and reduce the heat to low. Simmer the chicken gently for about 35 minutes, turning once, until very tender. Transfer the chicken to a cutting board and shred it with a fork into bite-sized pieces. Set the chicken aside.

5 Add the remaining 6 cups of chicken broth and the cilantro to the pot, season with salt, and lower the heat to medium. Simmer for about 20 minutes, stirring occasionally, until the broth has reduced slightly. Taste the soup and adjust the seasoning, if needed. Remove and discard the cilantro.

6 In a large skillet over medium-high heat, heat about 2 inches of avocado oil to 350°F. Set a wire rack over a baking sheet and place it nearby, for draining.

7 Working in batches, fry the tortilla strips for about 2 minutes, until just beginning to turn golden. Transfer the fried tortilla strips to the draining rack and sprinkle with salt. Repeat with the remaining tortilla strips.

8 **To serve:** Divide the soup among bowls and add a portion of the shredded chicken and a handful of the fried tortilla strips to each bowl. Top with generous amounts of avocado, cilantro, and radishes, plus lime wedges for squeezing.

FLAUTAS DE PAPA

MAKES 8 FLAUTAS | 1 HOUR 20 MINUTES | GF, DF, V

Grandma Campos's flautas set the gold standard that we're constantly aiming for. She would make hers with chicken and her famous flour tortillas, so we've adapted this recipe slightly to make them vegetarian and, if desired, to use tortillas made with grain-free flour. These flautas are also a great way to use up leftover cooked potatoes. As we like to say, if you got it, flauta it!

FOR THE SALSA ROJA

1 pound (4 or 5) Roma tomatoes, quartered

¼ cup chopped yellow onion

1 serrano chile, stemmed and seeded

1 garlic clove, peeled and smashed

½ teaspoon sea salt, plus more to taste

½ teaspoon dried Mexican oregano leaves or dried oregano leaves

FOR THE FLAUTAS

1½ pounds medium waxy potatoes (Yukon Gold or red), cut into large cubes

1 tablespoon plus ½ teaspoon sea salt

½ cup plus 1 tablespoon avocado oil, or your favorite oil for frying

2 garlic cloves, minced

1½ teaspoons ground cumin

Freshly ground black pepper

8 Siete Grain Free Almond Flour Tortillas, or tortillas of your choice

Cashew Crema (page 207)

1 cup shredded romaine lettuce

1 Make the salsa roja: In a small saucepan over medium heat, combine the tomatoes, onion, serrano, garlic, and salt with ½ cup of water. Bring to a simmer and partially cover the pan. Cook until the tomatoes are soft, about 15 minutes. Remove the pan from the heat. Carefully transfer the mixture to a high-speed blender and blend until smooth.

2 Add the salsa back to the pan over medium heat and crumble in the oregano by rubbing it against your hands. Cook, stirring occasionally, and reduce for 15 minutes. Taste and adjust the seasonings, if needed, and remove the pan from the heat.

3 Make the flautas: In a medium saucepan over medium-high heat, combine the potatoes, 1 tablespoon of the salt, and 1 quart of water. Bring to a simmer, partially cover, and cook until the potatoes are tender but some parts are still slightly

continued

firm, about 20 minutes. Drain the potatoes and wipe down the pot.

4 Heat 1 tablespoon of the oil in the same pot over low heat. Add the garlic and cumin and cook until fragrant, about 2 minutes. Add the potatoes and mash lightly with a potato masher or fork, breaking up any large chunks. Cook for 5 to 7 minutes, gently folding the garlic and cumin mixture into the potato. Season with the remaining ½ teaspoon of salt and some pepper. Remove the pan from the heat.

5 In a medium skillet over medium heat, heat the remaining ½ cup of avocado oil to 350°F.

6 The flautas are easiest to make if you start with warm tortillas. Warm them individually in a large sauté pan or cast-iron skillet over medium heat for 30 seconds, or microwave them for 30 seconds at a time, covered with a damp paper towel.

7 Add about ⅓ cup of the potato mixture to the center of a tortilla. Shape the mixture like a log, roll up the tortilla tightly around it, and secure with a toothpick so the filling stays in place. Set the flauta aside and repeat with the remaining tortillas and potato mixture.

8 Working in batches, fry the flautas until golden brown and crunchy on all sides, flipping occasionally, 5 to 6 minutes. Transfer the flautas to a plate lined with paper towels to drain and tent them with foil to keep warm.

9 Serve the flautas with the salsa roja, cashew crema, and lettuce.

SOPA DE FIDEO

SERVES 4 TO 6 | 40 MINUTES | GF, DF, V

Fideo "sopa," or "sopita," as many call it in Laredo, is a simple noodle soup. Some people say it's like a Mexican chicken noodle soup crossed with spaghetti because of its tomato-based, pepper-infused sauce and Mexican spices. Growing up, when we'd go shopping at our local grocery store, our mom would buy boxes of premade sopa de fideo that would come with dried noodles and a little seasoning packet. She'd dump it in boiling water, and we'd eagerly wait for it to cook because it was such a delicious treat. As adults, we still love this dish for its depth of flavor but also its relative simplicity to cook from scratch. There's nothing more to it than cooking the noodles in the flavorful tomato and adobo sauce until they're deliciously golden brown (Stir! Stir! Stir!) and then topping with queso panela and lime juice or enjoying with a side of warm tortillas.

¼ cup avocado oil, or neutral oil of your choice

6 ounces gluten-free spaghetti, broken into 1-inch pieces

1 white onion, finely diced

5 garlic cloves, minced

8 cups vegetable or chicken broth

1 cup tomato puree

½ bunch fresh cilantro, chopped

Sea salt and freshly ground black pepper

Lime wedges, for serving

1 In a large, heavy-bottomed pot over medium heat, heat the oil. Add the pasta and toss it in the hot oil, cooking until the pasta is fragrant and starts to color, about 1 minute. Add the onion and garlic and reduce the heat to medium-low. Cook, stirring, until the onions are translucent, about 3 minutes. Stir in the broth, tomato puree, and cilantro and season with salt and pepper. Increase the heat to medium-high and bring the soup to a boil, stirring constantly to keep the pasta from sticking to the bottom of the pot. Cook until the pasta is tender, which will vary depending on the brand.

2 Ladle the soup into bowls and serve with the lime wedges.

HEART OF PALM CEVICHE

SERVES 4 | 1 HOUR 30 MINUTES | GF, DF, V

Ceviche is one of Mexico's most beloved dishes, especially because so many states are close to the ocean and gulf. Normally you make it with fresh fish that's been "cooked" in an acid like fresh citrus juice, but we discovered that by swapping in fresh, briny hearts of palm, you get the same effect without the seafood. It's a beautiful, bright dish that's delicious with chips as a light lunch.

FOR THE CRISPY SPICED PEPITAS

¼ cup pumpkin seeds

1 teaspoon extra-virgin olive oil

¼ teaspoon ground cumin

¼ teaspoon ground paprika

Pinch of sea salt

FOR THE HEART OF PALM CEVICHE

1 (14.1-ounce) can whole hearts of palm, drained, cut lengthwise into quarters, and chopped into ½-inch pieces

¼ cup fresh lime juice (from about 2 limes)

¼ cup fresh orange juice (from about 1 orange)

2 tablespoons extra-virgin olive oil

¾ teaspoon sea salt

1 Roma tomato, chopped into ¼-inch pieces

½ avocado, diced

¼ cup minced red onion

¼ cup chopped fresh cilantro

Siete Tortilla Chips, or your favorite tortilla chips, for serving (optional)

1 Make the pepitas: Preheat the oven to 400°F. Line a baking sheet with parchment paper and set aside.

2 In a medium bowl, combine the pumpkin seeds, oil, cumin, paprika, and salt and toss to coat. Spread the mixture on the prepared baking sheet and bake for 8 to 10 minutes, stirring halfway through, until the seeds are golden and fragrant. Set aside to cool completely.

3 Make the ceviche: In a large bowl, add the chopped hearts of palm, lime juice, orange juice, olive oil, and salt and mix well to combine. Cover and marinate in the refrigerator for 1 hour.

4 Add the tomatoes, avocado, red onion, and cilantro to the heart of palm mixture and toss gently to combine. Sprinkle the crispy pepitas over the top and serve with tortilla chips, if desired.

CALDO DE POLLO

SERVES 6 TO 8 | 2 HOURS | GF, DF

Here's a simple staple among Mexican mothers that's as comforting to make as it is to eat. Simply add cabbage, potatoes, carrots, pulled chicken, and tomatoes to chicken broth, top with fresh lime, and you've got yourself a caldo de pollo well suited for a chilly day, or one curled up in bed.

The secret to making this soup is to bring together the broth first and then cook the vegetables in batches, making sure that each one is cooked to your liking before adding everything back into the broth. If you roll up a tortilla and dip it in the soup with each bite, then we'd say you're doing it right!

NOTE: Make sure your butcher includes the chicken neck, which will give your broth even more flavor.

---

1 (3- to 4-pound) chicken

½ medium white onion, peeled

1 tablespoon sea salt, plus more to taste

½ pound Roma tomatoes, cut into ¼-inch cubes

3 garlic cloves, finely chopped

2 dried bay leaves

1 pound waxy potatoes (such as Yukon Gold or red), scrubbed and quartered

2 medium carrots, peeled, cut lengthwise into quarters, quarters cut in half

4 ears of corn, shucked and cut into 3- to 4-inch cobs (optional)

2 medium zucchinis, halved lengthwise then quartered

Freshly ground black pepper

½ cup chopped fresh cilantro, for serving

2 limes, sliced into wedges, for serving

Warmed Siete Grain Free Cassava Flour Tortillas, or tortillas of your choice, for serving (optional)

Mexican Rice (page 134), for serving (optional)

1 In a large stockpot over medium-high heat, add the chicken, onion, and salt plus 4 quarts of water. Bring to a boil, then reduce the heat enough to maintain a gentle simmer. Add the tomatoes, garlic, and bay leaves and cook for 1 hour, skimming off any foam that rises to the top and discarding.

2 Keep the broth at a simmer as you carefully remove the chicken from the broth. Set aside to

continued

cool slightly and add the potatoes, carrots, and corn on the cob (if using). Partially cover the pot and simmer until the potatoes are tender but firm, 20 to 25 minutes. Add the zucchini and cook for an additional 10 minutes. When the chicken has cooled enough to handle, remove and discard the skin. Then remove the meat from the bones and pull it into shreds.

3 Remove the pot from the heat, cover, and let the caldo rest for 20 minutes. Remove the bay leaves and onion, if desired, and discard. Taste and season the soup with more salt and pepper, if needed.

4 Ladle the broth with the chicken and vegetables into shallow bowls and garnish with the cilantro and lime wedges on the side. Serve with tortillas and/or rice, if desired.

CALDO DE RES

SERVES 6 TO 8 | 2 HOURS 30 MINUTES | GF, DF

This soup is similar to caldo de pollo, but calls for beef chunks instead of chicken and includes a smorgasbord of different vegetables cut into large pieces. In South Texas, cold weather is caldo weather (which, as we mentioned before, is pretty much anything cooler than scorching), but we think this comforting, hearty soup is perfect for every season.

2 pounds beef chuck roast, cut into 1-inch cubes

1 pound bone-in short ribs, trimmed

1 tablespoon sea salt, plus more to taste

Freshly ground black pepper

½ medium yellow onion, finely chopped

2 garlic cloves, finely chopped

2 teaspoons dried Mexican oregano leaves or dried oregano leaves

1 small green cabbage, cut into 8 wedges

2 medium carrots, peeled and cut into 1-inch chunks

8 small Yukon Gold potatoes (about 1 pound), halved

3 ears of corn, husked and cut into thirds (optional)

3 medium zucchinis, cut into 1-inch rounds

Lime wedges, for serving

Warmed Siete Grain Free Almond Flour Tortillas, or tortillas of your choice, for serving (optional)

Mexican Rice (page 134), for serving (optional)

1 Generously season both the beef cubes and short ribs on all sides with salt and pepper.

2 In a large stockpot or Dutch oven over medium-high heat, add the beef cubes, short ribs, and 4 quarts of water. Bring the water to a boil and skim off any foam rising to the surface. Reduce the heat to medium and add the onion, garlic, oregano, and tablespoon salt. Partially cover and cook, adjusting the heat as needed to maintain a gentle simmer, until the meat is tender and easily pulls away from bone, 1 to 1½ hours.

3 Add the cabbage, carrots, potatoes, and corn (if using). Reduce the heat to low and cook until the vegetables are tender but still firm, 25 to 30 minutes. Add the zucchini and cook until tender, 10 more minutes. Taste and adjust the seasoning, if needed.

4 Ladle the caldo de res into deep bowls and serve with lime wedges, plus warm tortillas and Mexican rice, if desired.

RED PORK OR CHICKEN POZOLE

SERVES 6 TO 8 | 2 HOURS 45 MINUTES | GF, DF

If you ask any of us Garzas what dish we think of when it comes to special occasions, most of us will say "pozole." Whether it was holidays, birthdays, weddings, or *tornabodas*—the after-parties at weddings—we'd always look forward to a bowlful of our grandmother's hearty, soulful soup. Lucky for us, she'd make it in batches big enough to feed a village, ensuring there was more than enough to go around, and then enough for second (and third!) helpings. We created this recipe to help you skip waiting in a long line from the kitchen to the living room for a taste. Be sure not to overlook the toppings, which are just as essential to this dish as what goes into the soup itself!

FOR THE SOUP

1½ pounds pork shoulder, cut into 1-inch cubes, or 1½ pounds bone-in, skinless chicken thighs

1 medium white onion, peeled and left whole

4 garlic cloves, peeled and left whole

2 dried bay leaves

1 tablespoon dried Mexican oregano leaves or dried oregano leaves

Sea salt and freshly ground black pepper

3 dried guajillo chiles, stemmed and seeded

2 dried ancho chiles, stemmed and seeded

2 dried arbol chiles, stemmed

2 (15.5-ounce) cans hominy or chickpeas, drained and rinsed

FOR SERVING

½ small green cabbage head, very thinly sliced or shredded

6 radishes, thinly sliced

1 cup chopped fresh cilantro

½ cup finely diced white onion

Dried Mexican oregano leaves or dried oregano leaves

Lime wedges

1 In a large stockpot, add the pork or chicken, onion, garlic, bay leaves, and oregano and season with salt and pepper. Cover with 4 quarts of water and set the pot over medium-high heat. Bring to a boil, then reduce the heat to a steady simmer. Cook for 1 to 2 hours, until the meat is very tender. At the very end of cooking, add the guajillo, ancho, and arbol chiles and cook until just softened, 2 to 3 minutes.

2 In a high-speed blender, add 1 cup of the cooking broth, plus the onion and chiles from the pot, and blend until completely smooth.

Pour the mixture through a fine-mesh strainer straight back into the pozole.

3 Add the hominy to the pozole and return the pot to medium heat. Simmer for about 30 minutes to let the hominy soften and the flavors meld. Taste and adjust the seasoning.

4 Top servings of the pozole with the shredded cabbage, radishes, cilantro, onion, and oregano. Serve with lime wedges.

PIRATA TACOS

MAKES 8 TACOS | 45 MINUTES (PLUS 3-HOURS' MARINADE) | GF, DF [OPTION]

When we think of border-town food, our minds immediately go to pirata tacos. They're deliciously savory tacos that are traditionally made with two flour tortillas, refried beans, beef fajitas, and shredded cheddar cheese. As kids, we'd order these nearly every time we went out for lunch (especially at Taco Palenque, where they are a specialty), and to this day we urge friends visiting Laredo to make sure they try one while in town. But even if a trip to Texas isn't in your near future, we're happy to share our version with you, which our family enjoys as much as the original!

FOR THE MARINATED FAJITA

⅓ cup extra-virgin olive oil

⅓ cup fresh lime juice

⅓ cup coconut aminos

Zest of 1 orange

2 tablespoons red wine vinegar

1 tablespoon minced garlic

1½ teaspoons freshly ground black pepper

1 teaspoon sea salt, plus more to taste

½ teaspoon ground paprika

2 pounds skirt steak or 8 portobello mushroom caps

FOR THE TACOS

16 Siete Grain Free Cassava Flour Tortillas, or tortillas of your choice

2 cups Refried Beans (page 131), or store-bought, warmed

2 cups shredded cheddar cheese or dairy-free shredded cheese of your choice

Salsa Roja (page 45), for serving

Lime wedges, for serving

1 **Make the marinated fajita:** In a medium bowl, whisk together the oil, lime juice, coconut aminos, orange zest, vinegar, garlic, pepper, teaspoon salt, and paprika. Place the steak or mushroom caps in a zip-top plastic bag and add the marinade to the bag. Carefully push out any excess air and seal the bag. Marinate in the refrigerator for at least 3 hours and up to 12 hours, turning the bag every few hours.

2 Heat a grill or grill pan over medium-high heat. Remove the steak or mushrooms from the

continued

marinade, shaking off any excess. Dry the steak or mushrooms thoroughly with a paper towel and season with salt.

3 Grill for about 5 minutes per side for the steak, or to your desired doneness. Grill the mushroom caps for 5 to 8 minutes per side, until they've given up a good bit of their moisture and have reduced in size. Carve the steak or mushrooms into ½-inch-thick slices, making sure to cut against the grain of the steak.

4 **Assemble the tacos:** Char the tortillas using the residual heat from the grill or grill pan. For each taco, start with 2 stacked tortillas—the goal is to overfill these tacos. Spread a few tablespoons of the refried beans on the tortilla, followed by small handful of shredded cheese. Top generously with the sliced steak or mushrooms and serve with the salsa and lime wedges.

TOSTADAS DE ATÚN
(TUNA TOSTADAS)

MAKES 4 TOSTADAS | 45 MINUTES | GF, DF

We'll be the first to admit that we didn't grow up eating tuna tostadas—we were content with the simpler tostada varieties like bean and cheese. It wasn't until we got older that we learned to appreciate the seafood influence in our favorite dishes: As sushi restaurants gained popularity in our community, and as we started spending more time in Austin as adults, we began enjoying *mariscos*—seafood—on top of or alongside the Mexican staples we grew up eating, like tostadas. Topped with ahi tuna, thinly sliced avocado, and fried chile salsa, these tostadas go big on flavor but are still perfect for a light lunch.

½ cup avocado oil

4 Siete Grain Free Almond Flour Tortillas, or tortillas of your choice

½ cup packed fresh cilantro leaves

½ cup thinly sliced scallions, white and light green parts only

4 banana peppers, jarred (about 16 ounces)

¼ cup roughly chopped yellow onion

1 garlic clove, peeled and left whole

1 tablespoon plus 2 teaspoons fresh lime juice

½ teaspoon coconut sugar

¾ teaspoon sea salt, plus more to taste

½ pound sashimi-grade skinned tuna fillet, cut into ¼-inch cubes

1 teaspoon extra-virgin olive oil

½ avocado, thinly sliced, for serving

1 In a medium skillet over medium-low heat, heat ¼ cup of the avocado oil until shimmering.

2 Using tongs, gently lay one tortilla in the oil and fry for 1 minute per side, or until golden brown and crispy. Transfer the tostada to a paper towel–lined plate to drain. Repeat with the remaining tortillas, adding a bit more oil if the skillet starts to get dry.

3 In a medium bowl, cover the cilantro and scallions with cold water. Set aside.

4 Heat the remaining ¼ cup of avocado oil in a medium skillet over medium heat. Add the chiles and fry them for about 10 minutes, turning them often until blistered and golden brown on all sides. (You can use a screen or partially cover the skillet with a lid to keep the oil from splattering.)

continued

5 Transfer the fried chiles to a cutting board and remove the stems. In a blender, combine the chiles and all of their cooking oil, plus the onion, garlic, 1 tablespoon of the lime juice, the coconut sugar, ¼ teaspoon of the salt, and 2 tablespoons of water. Puree until smooth.

6 Drain the cilantro and green onions and return them to their bowl, along with the tuna, olive oil, the remaining 2 teaspoons of lime juice, and the remaining ½ teaspoon of salt. Toss to combine and adjust the seasoning with more salt, if needed.

7 Spread 1 tablespoon of the fried chile salsa on each tostada and top with ½ cup of the tuna mixture. Garnish with avocado slices.

TACOS DE PESCADO
(FISH TACOS)

MAKES 6 TACOS | 1 HOUR 15 MINUTES | GF, DF

The fish taco, in all its savory, crunchy, zesty glory, is a family favorite. We like to fry cod in a seasoned, tempura-style batter, which gives the fish an irresistibly light and crispy crunch with tons of flavor. All that's left to do is heap these tacos with avocado, creamy chipotle mayo, and a fresh slaw for the perfect bite.

FOR THE CABBAGE SLAW

¼ medium head green cabbage, cored and very thinly sliced

½ cup thinly sliced red onion

¼ cup chopped fresh cilantro

½ serrano chile, stemmed, seeded, and thinly sliced

Juice of 1 lime

¼ teaspoon sea salt

FOR THE BATTERED FISH

1½ cups cassava flour

2 tablespoons baking powder

1 (1.31-ounce) package Siete Taco Seasoning or Chorizo Seasoning, or taco seasoning of your choice

1 teaspoon sea salt

3 cups sparkling water, plus more if needed

Avocado oil, or your favorite oil, for frying

1 pound cod fillet, cut into ½-inch strips

FOR SERVING

6 to 12 Siete Grain Free Chickpea Flour Tortillas or Almond Flour Tortillas, or tortillas of your choice, warmed

1 cup Chipotle Mayo (page 212)

3 avocados, sliced

1 cup chopped fresh cilantro

4 limes, quartered

1 Make the cabbage slaw: In a medium bowl, toss together the cabbage, red onion, cilantro, serrano, lime juice, and salt. Use your hands or kitchen tongs to gently squeeze and massage the cabbage to help it break down and soften. Set aside.

2 Make the battered fish: In a medium bowl, whisk together the cassava flour, baking powder, taco seasoning, and salt until well combined. Add

continued

the sparkling water. The mixture will be like thick pancake batter, but thin enough to coat pieces of fish. Add an additional splash of sparkling water if the mixture is too thick.

3 In a cast-iron skillet over medium-high heat, heat about 1 inch of avocado oil to 350°F. Set a wire rack over a baking sheet and place it nearby, for draining.

4 Using tongs or a fork, coat each piece of fish in the batter and add it to the hot oil. Fry each piece of fish for 2 to 3 minutes, until golden and crispy. Transfer the fried fish to the rack and repeat with the remaining fish.

5 **Assemble the tacos:** Fill each tortilla with a small amount of the cabbage slaw and one or two pieces of battered fish. Drizzle with the chipotle mayo and top with a few avocado slices and cilantro. Serve with the lime quarters.

SHRIMP TOSTADAS

MAKES 8 TOSTADAS | 50 MINUTES | GF, DF

We've eaten a lot of tostadas over the years, but the first time we served these at a family dinner, a chorus of *mmms* filled the room. (And each time after, for that matter!) What's the secret to rendering everyone at the table speechless? It starts with pureeing shrimp with hot sauce—making a creamy shrimp paste to spread over tortillas—and then topping the tostadas with sesame seeds, fresh avocado, and slaw. The result is so good, we dare you to find the adjectives to describe it!

1 pound large shrimp, shelled and deveined

2 garlic cloves, peeled and smashed

2 tablespoons of your favorite hot sauce, plus more for serving

1 teaspoon sea salt

8 Siete Grain Free Cassava Flour Tortillas, or tortillas of your choice

¼ cup mixed black and white sesame seeds

½ cup avocado oil, or your favorite oil for frying

¾ cup Cashew Crema (page 207)

2 teaspoons fresh lime juice

¼ small red or green cabbage, cored and thinly sliced

¼ cup packed fresh cilantro leaves

1 In a food processor, combine the shrimp, garlic, hot sauce, and ½ teaspoon of the salt. Pulse until the mixture is a sticky but coarse paste, about 1 minute.

2 Using a rubber spatula, spread about ¼ cup of the shrimp mixture over each tortilla, evenly and to the edges. Sprinkle the sesame seeds over the shrimp paste and gently press down on the seeds so they adhere well to the mixture. Repeat with the remaining tortillas.

3 Heat the oil in a large nonstick skillet over medium heat. When the oil is shimmering, carefully add one tortilla, paste-side down, and cook until golden brown, 1 to 2 minutes. Use a pair of tongs to carefully flip and fry the other side until crispy like a chip, 1 to 2 more minutes. Transfer the fried shrimp tostadas to a plate lined with paper towels to drain. Repeat with the remaining tortillas.

4 In a large bowl, whisk together the cashew crema, lime juice, and the remaining ½ teaspoon of salt. Add the cabbage and cilantro and mix until the cabbage is well dressed and creamy.

5 Top the tostadas with the cabbage slaw and additional hot sauce.

FLAUTAS SUAVES

MAKES 8 FLAUTAS | 1 HOUR 15 MINUTES | GF, DF

Traditionally, flautas are crispy, but another way to enjoy them is soft and pillowy for *flautas sauves*, or soft flautas. For starters, the tortillas are dipped in hot oil, which lightly saturates them in fat and makes them instantly more pliable (and tasty). Then they are each filled with lightly seasoned shredded chicken, topped with perfectly sautéed onions, and drizzled along with a simple salsa verde. And, because most Mexican meals aren't complete without beans, they're accompanied by a hearty serving on the side that acts as a second sauce and dip for the flautas.

2 pounds boneless, skinless chicken breasts

2 small yellow onions: 1 peeled and halved, 1 sliced

1 dried bay leaf

1 tablespoon sea salt, plus more to taste

1 pound tomatillos, husks removed

¾ cup avocado oil, plus more as needed

2 garlic cloves, peeled and smashed

2 serrano chiles, stemmed, halved lengthwise, and seeded

½ cup fresh cilantro stems and leaves

8 Siete Grain Free Almond Flour Tortillas, or tortillas of your choice

4 cups Refried Beans (page 131), or store-bought, warmed, for serving

1 In a medium saucepan over medium-high heat, bring 6 cups of water to a simmer. Add the chicken, 1 onion half, the bay leaf, and 2 teaspoons of the salt. Reduce the heat to low, cover, and cook until the chicken is just cooked through, 12 to 15 minutes. Transfer the chicken to a medium bowl to let it cool enough to touch. Discard the onion, reserve 1½ cups of the broth, and save the remaining broth for another use.

2 Pull apart the chicken with your hands to shred it finely. Alternatively, you can shred the chicken in a stand mixer with the paddle attachment on low speed for about 1 minute. Add ½ cup of the broth to the chicken and mix to combine. Taste and season with salt as needed. Set aside.

3 In a medium saucepan over medium heat, add the tomatillos and the remaining 1 cup of the reserved chicken broth. Cover and simmer until the tomatillos are tender and cooked through, 4 to 6 minutes.

4 In a food processor, add half of the tomatillos, the remaining onion half, plus the garlic and serranos, and process until completely smooth. Add the remaining tomatillos, the cilantro, and ½ teaspoon of the remaining salt and pulse just a few times, until the mixture resembles a coarsely chopped salsa. Taste and adjust the salt as needed.

5 Heat ½ cup of the avocado oil in a large skillet over medium heat. Add the sliced onions and the remaining ½ teaspoon of salt. Cook until the onions are translucent and aromatic but not caramelized, 6 to 8 minutes. Transfer the onions to a small bowl and set aside.

6 Set the skillet over low-medium heat and add 2 tablespoons of the avocado oil. Using a pair of tongs, fry one tortilla at a time, dipping it in the oil and flipping it once or twice until the tortilla slightly puffs up and very lightly crisps, about 5 seconds per tortilla. Add another 2 tablespoons of oil if the skillet gets dry, usually after about 4 tortillas. Place the lightly fried tortillas on a plate and cover with foil to keep warm.

7 Add about ½ cup of the shredded chicken to each tortilla and tightly roll it up. Repeat with the remaining tortillas.

8 Top each flauta with a spoonful of the cooked onions. Serve with the refried beans and a small bowl of the salsa verde to pass around and pour all over the flautas right before eating.

TOSTADAS SIBERIAS

MAKES 4 TOSTADAS | 45 MINUTES | GF, DF, V (OPTION)

Tostadas siberias are quick and easy-to-make. They call for a crispy tostada base, guac, shredded chicken, and crema. Whether you're cooking for your family or entertaining a crowd, we recommend always serving these with escabeche. That way you can alternate between taking a bite out of the pickled jalapeño and carrots, and a bite of the tostada, enjoying both the rich and the acidic flavors together.

NOTE: Tostadas siberias are typically served with an extra tostada on top, which is why we call for 8 tortillas total in this recipe.

½ cup avocado oil

8 Siete Grain Free Almond Flour Tortillas, or tortillas of your choice

1 pound boneless, skinless chicken breast, or 2 cups store-bought rotisserie chicken, shredded, or Vegan Shredded "Meat" (page 223)

½ medium yellow onion, peeled

2 ½ teaspoons sea salt, plus more to taste

2 avocados, cubed

2 teaspoons fresh lime juice

1 cup Cashew Crema (page 207)

Escabeche (page 215), for serving (optional)

1 In a medium skillet over medium-low heat, heat ¼ cup of the oil until shimmering. Gently lay one tortilla in the hot oil and fry each side for 1 minute, until just golden, flipping once with tongs. Transfer the tostada to a paper towel–lined plate to drain and repeat with the remaining tortillas. Add the remaining ¼ cup of oil about halfway through the tortillas, or as needed if the skillet starts to look dry. Set the tostadas aside.

2 If you are using rotisserie chicken, skip this step. If you are cooking your chicken: In a medium saucepan over medium-high heat, bring 6 cups of water to a simmer. Add the chicken, onion, and 2 teaspoons of the salt. Cover, reduce the heat to low, and cook until the chicken is just cooked through, 12 to 15 minutes. Discard the onion, transfer the chicken to a medium bowl, and let it cool until just warm to the touch. Reserve ¼ cup of the broth and save the rest for another use.

continued

3 Pull apart the chicken with your hands until finely shredded. Alternatively, you can shred the chicken in a stand mixer fitted with the paddle attachment on low speed for about 1 minute. Pour the reserved ¼ cup of broth all over the chicken and mix to combine. Taste and season with salt as desired.

4 In a medium bowl, mash together the avocados, lime juice, and ½ teaspoon of the remaining salt until smooth

5 On each tostada, spread about 2 tablespoons of the avocado mixture and top with ½ cup of the shredded chicken and a generous spoonful of the cashew crema. Top with another tostada (if desired). Serve with the escabeche.

CALABAZA CON POLLO

SERVES 4 | 50 MINUTES | GF, DF

This dish is one of our favorite comfort foods, and it's an easy way to entice kids to eat their vegetables. The delicious smell emanating from the simmering pan of chicken and *calabacitas*, a variety of zucchini, puts everyone in the mood to dig in!

You can customize this dish to suit your dietary needs. For example, you can swap in Mexican Cauliflower Rice (page 135) for the traditional rice, or omit the chicken. If you decide to go meatless, we recommend serving the dish with some Cashew Crema (page 207) for extra richness.

2 tablespoons avocado oil

1 small yellow onion, finely chopped

4 garlic cloves, minced

1½ teaspoons ground cumin

1 pound boneless, skinless chicken thighs, sliced into ½-inch strips

½ teaspoon sea salt, plus more to taste

Freshly ground black pepper

1 (14.5-ounce) can diced tomatoes

1 pound calabacitas or zucchini, trimmed, halved, and sliced into half-moons

1 serrano chile, stemmed, seeded, and minced

Mexican Rice (page 134), for serving

8 Siete Foods Grain Free Almond Flour Tortillas or tortillas of your choice, warmed, for serving

1 Heat the oil in a large skillet over medium heat. Add the onion, garlic, and cumin and cook until the onion is translucent and fragrant, 5 to 7 minutes.

2 Season the chicken with salt and pepper, add it to the skillet, and cook until the chicken is no longer pink on the outside, about 5 minutes. (The chicken will continue to cook through with the rest of the vegetables.)

3 Increase the heat to high and add the tomatoes with their juice, the zucchini, serrano, ½ teaspoon of salt, and pepper to taste. Cover and cook for about 5 minutes, stirring once, until the tomatoes and zucchini release most of their juices. Reduce the heat to medium and uncover to let the liquid reduce to a saucy consistency, about 10 more minutes. Taste and adjust the seasonings as necessary.

4 Serve with Mexican rice and warm tortillas.

SHRIMP COCKTAIL

SERVES 4-6 | 35 MINUTES | GF, DF

Venture into any seafood restaurant by the south Texas border and you're bound to see a whole bunch of tables set with an extra-large margarita glass at the center. Upon closer inspection, you'd find that these glasses aren't strictly for adult beverages. They're filled with shrimp cocktail: cooked shrimp, cucumber, and avocado marinating in a hot sauce–spiked cocktail sauce. It's a great dish for sharing as an appetizer or enjoying with a side of crackers or your favorite tortilla chips.

NOTE: This recipe is great for customizing as you like it. Add more lime juice or hot sauce to the cocktail sauce to suit your preferences.

---

1 pound large cooked peeled shrimp, cut into ½-inch pieces

1 Roma tomato, diced

1 cup diced cucumber

¼ cup finely chopped red or yellow onion

¼ cup fresh lime juice

1 serrano chile, stemmed, seeded, and finely chopped

1½ teaspoons sea salt

1 teaspoon freshly ground black pepper

½ cup tomato juice

½ cup ketchup

¼ cup clam juice

¼ cup your favorite hot sauce, plus more to taste

1 tablespoon fresh lemon juice

1 tablespoon coconut aminos

¼ teaspoon garlic powder

1 cup chopped fresh cilantro leaves and stems, plus more for serving

1 avocado, diced

Siete Sea Salt Grain Free Tortilla Chips, or tortilla chips of your choice, for serving

1 In a large bowl, toss together the shrimp, tomato, cucumber, onion, lime juice, serrano, salt, and pepper. Set aside in the refrigerator while you make the cocktail sauce.

2 In a medium bowl, whisk together the tomato juice, ketchup, clam juice, hot sauce, lemon juice, coconut aminos, and garlic powder until smooth. Add the cilantro and whisk again to combine.

3 Pour the cocktail sauce over the shrimp mixture and fold gently to combine. Cover and refrigerate for 1 hour before serving.

4 Just before serving, gently fold in the avocado. Serve with the tortilla chips.

3

SNACKS/BOTANAS

Ever since we were kids, our family has loved a good midday (and, on occasion, late-night, post-breakfast, pre-dinner) snack. There were crispy potato chips drenched in hot sauce and lime juice from our local convenience store; buttery, cheesy elotes preparados complete with spicy chile sauce from street vendors; fresh fruit cups topped with chamoy; and Grandma Campos's fresh tortillas with butter. As we've learned more about how food affects the way we feel, we've challenged ourselves to find ways to re-create these nostalgic treats without compromising on flavor or convenience. With simple ingredient swaps, we've been able to do just that, from refreshing homemade mango raspas to fried pickled jalapeños and carrots to classic Mexican street corn.

FRIED PICKLED JALAPEÑOS AND CARROTS WITH DAIRY-FREE RANCH

SERVES 2 TO 4 | 40 MINUTES | GF, DF, V

We'll see your fried pickles and raise you these fried pickled jalapeños and carrots! This spicy spin on a county fair classic is a snack or appetizer you can bet on for your next BBQ or carne asada. It's basically fried escabeche, with a batter that gets its light and airy texture from cassava flour. We recommend serving it with dairy-free ranch dipping sauce for a taste of finger food at its finest!

FOR THE RANCH DIPPING SAUCE

⅔ cups dairy-free plain yogurt

⅓ cup vegan mayonnaise

Juice of 2 limes

1 garlic clove, grated

1 teaspoon onion powder

1 teaspoon dried dill

1 teaspoon dried parsley

½ bunch fresh cilantro, chopped (optional)

Pinch of sea salt

FOR THE FRIED PICKLED JALAPEÑOS AND CARROTS

1 (12-ounce) can sliced pickled jalapeños and carrots

2 cups sparkling water

1¼ cups cassava flour

1 tablespoon your favorite hot sauce

½ tablespoon dried cilantro

½ teaspoon sea salt

¼ teaspoon freshly ground black pepper

Avocado oil, or your favorite oil for frying

1 In a medium bowl, whisk together the yogurt, mayonnaise, lime juice, garlic, onion powder, dill, and parsley. Make it a cilantro ranch by adding the chopped cilantro, if desired.

2 Make the fried pickled jalapeños and carrots: Drain the jalapeños and carrots thoroughly and spread them across a few layers of paper towels to dry.

3 In a medium bowl, whisk together the sparkling water, cassava flour, hot sauce, cilantro, salt, and pepper.

4 In a large, high-sided skillet or Dutch oven, heat 2 inches of oil over medium-high heat to 375°F. Set a baking sheet or plate lined with paper towels near the stove for draining.

5 Use a fork to quickly dip each jalapeño and carrot piece in the batter and fry until crispy, 5 to 8 minutes. Transfer to the prepared baking sheet to drain.

6 Serve the fried jalapeños and carrots immediately with the ranch.

MANGO RASPAS

SERVES 8 | 4 HOURS 15 MINUTES | GF, DF, V

In some cities he might be known as "the Ice Cream Man," but in South Texas, the man who drives around selling frozen treats is more often known as "the Raspa Man." When we heard the familiar tune jingling down the block, our family would run cheering, "The Raspa Man is coming!" as the truck stocked with snacks, paletas, and raspas drove up to our house. *Raspas* are Mexican shaved ices, which get drizzled and covered with all kinds of flavored syrups—cherry, raspberry, pineapple, chamoy, tamarindo, and our favorite, mango. We still can't eat one without thinking about hot summer days and the truck that brought us a much-needed treat.

1½ pounds fresh mango

½ cup agave nectar

Juice of 2 limes

¼ teaspoon sea salt

Chamoy, homemade (page 209), or store-bought, for serving (optional)

1 In a blender, combine the mango, agave, lime juice, and salt with 1 cup of water. Blend until the mixture is completely smooth. Pour the mixture into an 8 x 8-inch baking dish and carefully transfer it to the freezer. Freeze until the mixture is frozen solid, 3 to 4 hours.

2 Use a fork to rake and scrape the frozen mango mixture into crystals, like shaved ice. Divide the raspa among bowls and serve. To make ahead, transfer the raspa to an airtight, freezer-safe container and store in the freezer until ready to serve.

3 Serve drizzled with chamoy, if desired.

PAPITAS PREPARADAS

SERVES 1 | 10 MINUTES | GF, DF, V

This is our brother Miguel's favorite snack: a mound of potato chips slathered in lime juice, hot sauce, and crema. It's usually sold by street carts at fairs, in Mexican mercados, and in snack shops across Laredo, but it's simple enough for you to make at home. This updated version swaps in a cashew-based crema instead of cheese-based sauce and uses kettle-cooked chips.

1 (5.5-ounce) bag Siete Kettle Cooked Potato Chips, or kettle-cooked potato chips of your choice

Juice of 1 lime

2 tablespoons Cashew Crema (page 207)

Your favorite hot sauce

In a large bowl, toss the chips with the lime juice, crema, and hot sauce. Alternatively, you can combine the toppings and chips right in the bag, hold the bag closed, and shake vigorously to combine.

ELOTES PREPARADOS

MAKES 4 ELOTES | 30 MINUTES | DF, V

Also called "Mexican Street Corn," this dish is a popular snack sold by street vendors in Mexico and South Texas. It usually gets its decadence from layers of cheese and mayonnaise, but ours uses cashew crema and a vegan cotija cheese that is equally tangy, savory, and satisfying thanks to olives and nutritional yeast!

NOTE: Enjoy yours directly off of the cob, or slice off the kernels and assemble in a cup!

FOR THE VEGAN COTIJA

2 teaspoons nutritional yeast

½ teaspoon sea salt

½ teaspoon onion powder

4 green olives (such as Castelvetrano), pitted and finely chopped

½ cup super-fine almond flour

FOR THE ELOTES

4 ears of corn, husks intact

1 cup Cashew Crema (page 207)

1 tablespoon fresh lime juice

1 recipe Chile-Lime Seasoning (page 210)

2 limes, sliced into wedges, for serving

1 Make the vegan cotija: In a spice grinder or food processor, add the nutritional yeast, salt, and onion powder and pulse until combined. Add the olives and pulse until the olives are ground and the mixture has the texture of wet sand. Transfer the mixture to a medium bowl and add the almond flour. Use a fork to fluff and combine the mixture. Set aside.

2 Make the elotes: Preheat a grill or cast-iron skillet over medium-high heat.

3 Place the ears of corn, still in their husks, directly over the fire. Cover the grill or pan and cook the corn for about 5 minutes per side, rotating until the husks are evenly charred, about 20 minutes total.

4 In a small bowl, whisk together the cashew crema and lime juice. Cover and chill the crema mixture until ready to serve.

5 Pull back the corn husks and the silk, leaving the husks attached to the base of the cob. Using a pastry brush or a butter knife, spread the cashew crema mixture on the corn. Transfer the corn to a platter and sprinkle generously with the vegan cotija and chile-lime seasoning on all sides. Serve with the lime wedges for squeezing over the corn.

FRUIT CUPS

SERVES 8 TO 10 | 20 MINUTES | GF, DF, V

Perhaps our favorite way to eat fruit—next to paletas and aguas frescas—this snack reminds us of the vibrant varieties of fruit spears available in Mexican mercados, like pineapple, watermelon, cantaloupe, jicama, and mango. This combination of fresh fruit, chile powder, lime, and tangy chamoy is sold by cart vendors in the street or served on giant platters at birthday parties and family gatherings.

2 large mangos, peeled and cut lengthwise into ½-inch-wide spears

½ medium pineapple (about 1½ pounds), peeled, cored, and cut lengthwise into ½-inch-wide spears

¼ small seedless watermelon (about 1¼ pounds), peeled and cut lengthwise into ½-inch-wide spears

1 cucumber, peeled and cut lengthwise into ½-inch spears

¼ cantaloupe (about 1¼ pounds), peeled and cut into ½-inch cubes

2 limes, cut into wedges

½ cup Chamoy (page 209), or store-bought, plus more for serving

¼ cup Chile-Lime Seasoning (page 210), or store-bought, plus more for serving

Using a tall glass for each serving, arrange a few spears each of the mango, pineapple, watermelon, and cucumber. Nestle a few cubes of cantaloupe between the spears. Squeeze lime juice over the fruit to taste and drizzle 1 tablespoon or more of the chamoy into each glass. Season with a sprinkle of the chile-lime seasoning and serve with more chamoy on the side for dipping.

FRESAS CON CREMA

SERVES 4 | 1 HOUR 30 MINUTES | GF, DF, V

Texas gets *hot*. And for some reason, hot days under the Texas sun call for a very specific remedy when the day is done and it's time to kick your feet up: *fresas con crema,* or strawberries with whipped cream. We make ours with a sweet, dairy-free cashew crema, but you can use dairy whipped cream if you prefer. Be sure to look for the biggest, juiciest berries you can find for this dish, since they are the star of the show!

FOR THE DAIRY-FREE CREMA

2 cups raw unsalted cashews

3 tablespoons fresh lemon juice

3 tablespoons maple syrup, plus more for finishing

½ teaspoon vanilla extract

¼ teaspoon sea salt

TO ASSEMBLE

1 pound strawberries, rinsed, hulled, and halved or sliced, if large

½ cup Siete Mexican Shortbread Cookies, or shortbread cookies of your choice, crushed into small pieces (optional)

1 Make the crema: In a medium saucepan over high heat, bring 6 cups of water to a rolling boil. Add the cashews, reduce the heat to medium, and cook at a rapid simmer for 20 minutes. Drain the cashews and rinse well under running water.

2 Transfer the cashews to a high-speed blender and add the lemon juice, maple syrup, vanilla, and salt plus 1 cup of water. Puree until completely smooth and creamy, 1 to 2 minutes. Transfer the crema to a small bowl and cover. Chill in the refrigerator for at least 1 hour, or until ready to serve.

3 Assemble: Add a layer of the strawberries to each of 4 ramekins or small bowls. Top with a spoonful of the cashew crema and repeat with another layer of strawberries. Continue until each ramekin has 3 or 4 layers of strawberries. Arrange the remaining strawberries on top and drizzle with more maple syrup and the crushed shortbread cookies, if using.

4

DINNER/CENA

No matter how busy our days were, our family always came together for dinner at the end of the day. We'd sit in our self-assigned seats, and since we often had friends over, we'd pull up some extra chairs from all over the house, scooching and sliding around so that everyone could fit. Some nights we'd have quesadillas, other nights we'd dig into a giant batch of warm spaghetti noodles with savory red tomato meat sauce, and on our favorite evenings, our mom would make milanesa. Regardless of what was on our plate, dinner was the product of her signature style of cooking: doing more with less.

We've carried this style of cooking into our own kitchens—resourcefulness and innovation that turn humble ingredients into unforgettable meals; unfussy, freeform ways of creating recipes; generosity and care that infuse every meal, ensuring everyone walks away with a full belly and a full heart.

In this chapter, you'll find recipes that work as convenient weeknight staples, like frijolizzas and quesadillas, in addition to dishes that may inspire you to get out your serving platters in the name of feeding a crowd, such as chicken with mole and enchiladas. Whichever recipe you land on, we hope it's just what you need to approach family-style dinners with a little less time for worry, and a little more time for love.

ENCHILADAS THREE WAYS

The expression "the whole enchilada"—as in, everything you could ask for—certainly rings true to us, as enchiladas feature everything we could possibly want in one dish. Enchiladas traditionally come in many variations, and these are some of our favorites: enchiladas verdes (enchiladas with tomatillo-based sauce), enchiladas de res (enchiladas with a guajillo chile–based sauce), and enchiladas suizas (enchiladas in a tomatillo-crema blend). In every case, you are looking at a combination of delicious fillings bundled up in a tortilla and smothered with a delicious sauce. Since many enchiladas contain cheese or crema, we were determined to do them justice when creating our very own dairy-free versions. We think we accomplished that goal—these recipes really are the whole enchilada.

ENCHILADAS VERDES

MAKES 8 ENCHILADAS | 1 HOUR 30 MINUTES | GF, DF, V [OPTION]

Enchiladas verdes get their bright and tangy flavoring from one of our favorite ingredients, the *tomatillo*, or Mexican husk tomato. Unlike its sweeter red doppelganger, the tomatillo is not actually a tomato but a type of gooseberry that is tarter than a tomato. They're great in salsas, stews, and soups, and each time we use them in this recipe, we can't help but think the best things in life are green.

NOTE: Unlike the other two enchilada recipes, this version calls for frying the tortillas before assembling the enchiladas. You could skip this step— or you could add it when making either of the other variations*

FOR THE ENCHILADA SAUCE*

½ pound tomatillos, husks removed and rinsed

2 garlic cloves, peeled and left whole

½ serrano chile, halved lengthwise, stems and seeds removed

½ white onion

¾ cups chicken broth

*You can also substitute this with 1 jar of Siete Green Enchilada Sauce

FOR THE ENCHILADAS

1 tablespoon plus 3 teaspoons avocado oil, or your favorite oil for frying, plus more as needed

3 cups store-bought rotisserie chicken, shredded, or Vegan Shredded "Meat" (page 223)

8 Siete Grain Free Cassava Flour Tortillas, or tortillas of your choice

1 cup Cashew Crema (page 207)

Cilantro, for garnish

1 Preheat the oven to 350°F. Spread 1 teaspoon of avocado oil into an 8 x 8-inch baking dish.

2 Make the enchilada sauce by combining the tomatillos, garlic, serrano, onion, and chicken broth in a medium saucepan over medium heat. Cover and simmer until the tomatillos and onion are tender and cooked through, 8 to 10 minutes. Alternatively, use one 15-ounce jar Siete Green Enchilada Sauce and skip step 3, step 4, and step 5; proceed with the recipe.

3 Transfer tomatillo mixture along with the cooking liquid and 1 teaspoon of salt to a blender. Puree until completely smooth.

4 Add 2 teaspoons of oil to a medium saucepan over low-medium heat. When the oil is shimmering, carefully add the enchilada sauce to the pan. Lower the heat to low and simmer gently, cooking until the sauce slightly thickens, 5 to 8 minutes. Keep warm at the lowest setting until ready to assemble the enchiladas.

5 Add 1 tablespoon of avocado oil to a medium skillet over low-medium heat. Using a pair of tongs, lightly dip one tortilla at a time in the oil, flipping it once or twice until the tortilla slightly puffs up but does not get crispy, about 5 to 10 seconds per tortilla. Add more oil as needed if the skillet gets dry. Place the lightly fried tortillas on a plate covered with foil to keep them warm as you work through the rest of the tortillas.

6 Pour ¼ cup of the enchilada sauce onto the baking dish. Reserve the rest of the sauce for assembly.

7 Add about ⅓ cup of shredded chicken to each tortilla and tightly roll. Repeat, lining up enchiladas in the baking dish.

8 Pour the rest of the sauce all over the enchiladas. Cover the dish with aluminum foil and place in the oven. Bake until the sauce is bubbly, 15 to 20 minutes.

9 Remove the dish from the oven and uncover. Drizzle the cashew crema on the enchiladas and garnish with cilantro.

ENCHILADAS DE RES

SERVES 4 | 1 HOUR 30 MINUTES | GF, DF [OPTION], V

While there are a 'lada different varieties of enchiladas out there, this recipe is one of our favorites. It's got a smoky and warm tomato-chile paste that we love pairing with savory ground beef and smothering in queso and crema.

FOR THE ENCHILADA SAUCE*

1 medium tomato, halved lengthwise

3 guajillo chiles, stems and seeds removed

2 ancho chiles, stems and seeds removed

¼ cup chopped yellow onions

1 teaspoon ground cumin

2 garlic cloves, peeled and left whole

½ teaspoon dried oregano

½ teaspoon apple cider vinegar

2 teaspoons coconut sugar

2 teaspoons sea salt

*You can also substitute this with 1 jar of Siete Red Enchilada Sauce

FOR THE ENCHILADAS

3 teaspoons avocado oil

1 tablespoon tomato paste

1 pound ground beef or Vegan Ground "Meat" (page 222)

8 Siete Foods Grain Free Almond Flour Tortillas, or tortillas of your choice

Shredded Mexican cheese blend (optional)

FOR THE MEAT SEASONING*

1 tablespoon mild chili powder

1 teaspoon garlic powder

1 teaspoon onion powder

½ teaspoon smoked paprika

1 ½ teaspoons coconut sugar

*You can also substitute this with 1 package Siete Mild Taco Seasoning

1 Make the enchilada sauce by combining tomato, guajillos, anchos, and 2 cups of water in a small saucepan. Bring to a boil over medium-low heat, pressing on the chiles to submerge them. Partially cover the pan and cook until the tomato is bursting and the chiles are soft, 10 minutes. Turn off the heat, cover, and let stand for 10 minutes. Alternatively, use one 15-ounce jar Siete Red Enchilada Sauce and skip step 1 and step 2; proceed with the recipe.

2 Transfer mixture along with ¾ cup of the cooking liquid to a blender. Discard the rest of the liquid. Add onion, cumin, garlic cloves, oregano, apple cider vinegar, 2 teaspoons coconut sugar, and 2 teaspoons salt. Purée until smooth. Transfer to a medium bowl.

3 Preheat the oven to 350°F. Spread 1 teaspoon of avocado oil into an 8 x 11-inch baking dish.

4 For the meat filling, heat 1 teaspoon of avocado oil in a large skillet over medium-high heat. Add tomato paste and cook until the paste starts to darken, 3 to 5 minutes.

5 Add beef and ¼ teaspoon of salt; break up beef with a wooden spoon and mix the tomato paste; then spread it out to create a single layer. Cook until the beef is lightly browned and crisp, about 5 minutes. Alternatively, you may also use one package Siete Mild Taco Seasoning to season the beef; omit the tomato paste on step 5. Substitute ingredients on step 6 and add Siete Mild Taco Seasoning instead along with ⅓ cup of water to season the beef. Proceed with cooking the beef until a sauce forms in step 6.

6 Add chili powder, garlic powder, onion powder, smoked paprika, coconut sugar, 1¼ teaspoon salt and ¼ cup of water all over the beef. Cook until the beef is slightly saucy and cooked through, 5 to 7 minutes. Taste and adjust seasonings. Remove from the heat.

7 Pour ½ cup of the enchilada sauce to lightly cover the bottom of the greased baking dish. Reserve the remaining sauce.

8 Preheat a large pan or a comal (griddle) over medium-high heat. Warm up the tortillas, 5 to 10 seconds per side, flipping them once or twice. Repeat with the remaining tortillas and keep them warm inside a foil packet or a cloth napkin.

9 Add ½ cup of the taco ground beef to each tortilla and tightly roll. Repeat with remaining tortillas, adding them to the greased baking dish.

10 Pour the remaining enchilada sauce all over the enchiladas. Top with shredded cheese, if desired. Cover the dish with aluminum foil and bake enchiladas for 15 to 20 minutes, until the sauce is bubbling and cheese is melted.

11 Uncover and divide enchiladas among plates. If desired, top with your favorite dairy-free crema and garnish with cilantro.

ENCHILADAS SUIZAS

SERVES 4 | 1 HOUR 30 MINUTES | GF, DF [OPTION], V [OPTION]

Enchiladas suizas are usually filled with chicken and topped with a blended salsa of tomatillos and crema, plus a generous amount of grated cheese, and to finish it off, *more crema*. We've given it a dairy-free spin, and while we used to circulate this as a secret recipe to friends and family, we've decided we can no longer keep it to ourselves*

FOR THE ENCHILADA SAUCE*

2 cups chicken or vegetable broth

½ pound tomatillos, husks removed and rinsed

½ white onion

2 garlic cloves, peeled and left whole

½ serrano chile, halved lengthwise, stems and seeds removed

½ cup Cashew Crema (page 207) or 8-ounces plain cream cheese, plus more crema for serving

¼ cup of coconut milk

*You can also substitute this with 1 jar of Siete Green Enchilada Sauce

FOR THE ENCHILADAS

3 teaspoons avocado oil, or your favorite oil for frying

4 cups store-bought rotisserie chicken, shredded, or Vegan Shredded "Meat" (page 223),

⅓ cup packed fresh cilantro leaves, plus more for garnish

8 Siete Foods Grain Free Almond Flour Tortillas, or tortillas of your choice

¼ cup red onion thinly sliced into rings

1 Preheat the oven to 350°F. Spread 1 teaspoon of avocado oil into a 13-by-9-by-2-inch casserole dish.

2 Make the enchilada sauce by combining chicken broth, tomatillos, onion, garlic and serrano in a medium saucepan over medium heat. Cover and simmer until the tomatillos and onion are tender and cooked through, 8 to 10 minutes. Alternatively, use one 15-ounce jar Siete Green Enchilada Sauce. Alternatively if using Siete Enchilada Sauce, skip steps 3-6, then proceed with the recipe.

3 Transfer tomatillo mixture along with cooking liquid and 1 teaspoon of salt to a blender. Puree until completely smooth.

4 Add 2 teaspoons oil to a medium saucepan over low-medium heat. When the oil is shimmering, carefully add the enchilada sauce to the pan. Lower the heat to low and simmer gently, cooking until the sauce slightly thickens, 5 to 8 minutes.

5 Combine the enchilada sauce or, if using, Siete Green Enchilada Sauce, ½ cup cashew crema, coconut milk, cilantro, and ½ teaspoon of salt in a blender. Puree until smooth.

6 Pour ¾ cup enchilada sauce into the casserole dish and spread evenly over the bottom.

7 On a comal (griddle) over medium heat, warm up tortillas for 30 seconds on each side.

8 Add about ⅓ cup of shredded chicken (or non-dairy filling, if using) to each tortilla and tightly roll. Repeat, lining up enchiladas in the baking dish.

9 Pour the rest of the sauce all over the enchiladas. Cover the dish with aluminum foil and place in the oven. Bake until the sauce is bubbly, 15 to 20 minutes.

10 Remove the dish from the oven and uncover. Drizzle cashew crema on the enchiladas and garnish with onion rings and cilantro.

CARNE GUISADA

SERVES 4 | 2 HOURS 30 MINUTES | GF, DF

When Grandma Campos cooked, she would "guisada todo." In other words, she'd make pretty much anything *guisada*, or stew-style. But her specialty was carne guisada, a juicy, savory mix of beef and potatoes. We recommend serving as she would, with tortillas to mop up the stew.

NOTE: This stew has a longer cooking time because this cut of meat needs low and slow cooking to become nice and tender.

2 pounds beef chuck roast, cut into 1-inch cubes

Sea salt and freshly ground black pepper

¼ cup extra-virgin olive oil, plus more if needed

1 large yellow onion, thinly sliced

6 garlic cloves, minced

1 cup tomato puree

2 cups beef broth or water

2 dried bay leaves

½ bunch fresh cilantro

½ cup chopped fresh cilantro, for serving

Mexican Rice (page 134), for serving (preferably hot)

Refried Beans (page 131), or store-bought, warmed, for serving

Siete Grain Free Almond Flour Tortillas, or tortillas of your choice, warmed, for serving

1 Pat the beef dry with paper towels. In a large bowl, season the beef generously with salt and pepper and toss to coat.

2 In a large, heavy-bottomed pot over medium-high heat, heat the oil. Working in batches, sear the beef cubes on at least two sides, 3 to 4 minutes per side, until browned and starting to crisp at the edges. Transfer the browned beef to a plate.

3 If the pot looks dry, add another splash of olive oil. Add the onion and cook, stirring, until translucent, about 5 minutes. Add the garlic and cook until just fragrant, about 30 seconds. Pour in the tomato puree and broth and mix to combine. Add the bay leaves and ½ bunch cilantro (leaving the bunch whole). Bring the mixture to a simmer and season with salt and pepper.

4 Cover the pot and reduce the heat to medium-low. Cook for 1½ to 2 hours, until the beef is very tender. Taste and adjust the seasoning with salt and pepper, if needed.

5 Top with the chopped cilantro and serve alongside rice, refried beans, and warm tortillas.

CHICKEN WITH MOLE

SERVES ABOUT 6 | 1 HOUR 40 MINUTES | GF, DF

Mole is a rich, complex sauce that has more unique twists than a telenovela. Every family has their own special version using various types of chiles and chocolate blends. While mole is notorious for being a labor of love and requiring many, many ingredients, our family's recipe simplifies the process and still packs mole's signature flavor. It's perfect for simmering chicken in and serving with plenty of rice and—you guessed it—tortillas!

FOR THE CHICKEN

2 to 3 pounds bone-in chicken breasts and whole legs

½ medium white onion, peeled

3 garlic cloves, finely chopped

2 dried bay leaves

1½ teaspoons sea salt

FOR THE MOLE ALMENDRADO

½ pound Roma tomatoes or other small-medium tomatoes

¼ cup roughly chopped yellow onion

2 garlic cloves, unpeeled

3 dried ancho chiles (about ½ ounce), stemmed and seeded

½ cup blanched almonds

2 whole cloves

1 (1-inch) cinnamon stick

3 Medjool dates, pitted

4½ cups reserved chicken broth

1 tablespoon avocado oil

2 ounces 60 to 70 percent dark chocolate, coarsely chopped

2 tablespoons coconut sugar, plus more if needed

½ teaspoon sea salt, plus more if needed

1 tablespoon toasted sesame seeds

FOR SERVING

Mexican Rice (page 134)

Siete Grain Free Almond Flour Tortillas, or tortillas of your choice, warmed

1 Make the chicken: In a large stockpot over high heat, combine 4 quarts of water with the chicken breasts and legs, the onion, garlic, bay leaves, and salt. Bring to a boil, reduce the heat to medium, and maintain a gentle simmer for 15 minutes. Skim off any foam that rises to the top.

continued

Cover and remove the pot from the heat until ready to serve. Reserve enough broth to make the mole and save the remaining broth for another use.

2 **Make the mole almendrado:** In a dry cast-iron skillet or comal over medium heat, add the tomatoes, onion, and garlic. Cook, turning the vegetables a few times, until they are blackened in spots and the tomatoes start to burst, 10 to 15 minutes. Transfer the vegetables to a medium bowl. Peel the garlic once it is cool enough to handle.

3 In the same pan over medium heat, add the anchos, almonds, cloves, and cinnamon stick. Toast everything, stirring frequently to prevent burning, until the almonds are golden brown, 5 to 7 minutes.

4 In a small saucepan over high heat, add 2 cups of the reserved broth, the toasted anchos, and dates, and bring to a boil. Remove the pan from the heat, cover, and let it sit until the chiles and dates are soft and pulpy, about 10 minutes.

5 Transfer the chiles, dates, and 1 cup of their cooking broth to a blender along with the tomatoes, onion, garlic, almonds, cloves, cinnamon stick, and remaining 2 cups of broth and blend until completely smooth. Pass the sauce through a fine-mesh strainer into a bowl, discarding the solids.

6 Heat the avocado oil in a medium saucepan over low heat. Add the mole, chocolate, coconut sugar, and salt and stir until the chocolate melts. Simmer the mole gently for the flavors to meld, about 20 minutes. The texture of the mole should be slightly thicker than heavy cream. If it's too thick, add a splash more broth. Taste and adjust the seasonings, adding more coconut sugar or salt if needed.

7 When ready to serve, transfer the chicken to a plate and remove the skin. You can separate the drumsticks from the thighs or keep the legs whole and slice the breast if you wish.

8 Serve the chicken in shallow bowls and cover it with the mole almendrado. Garnish with the sesame seeds and serve with Mexican rice and warm tortillas.

BEEF SALPICÓN

SERVES 4 | 1 HOUR | GF, DF

We can't recall a single family gathering that didn't feature a platter of piping hot, perfectly tender beef, braised to perfection. In this recipe, we've shredded and marinated beef in a serrano-lime dressing along with crisp, fresh veggies. Pile it on top of a crispy tostada along with a few slices of avocado, and taste what it's like to be at our table for this savory tradition.

1½ pounds beef flank steak, cut in half

1 white onion, peeled and halved

3 garlic cloves, peeled and left whole

2 dried bay leaves

2 teaspoons sea salt

¼ cup fresh lime juice

3 serrano chiles, stemmed, seeded, and finely minced

1 teaspoon dried Mexican oregano leaves or dried oregano leaves

Freshly ground black pepper

¼ cup extra-virgin olive oil

3 cups shredded romaine lettuce

1 bunch of radishes, thinly sliced

½ cup roughly chopped fresh cilantro leaves

8 Siete Grain Free Almond Flour Tortillas, or store-bought tostadas, for serving

1 avocado, sliced

1 Preheat oven to 350°F. In a large stockpot, combine the steak, 1 onion half, the garlic, bay leaves, 1 teaspoon of the salt, and 2 quarts of water. Set the pot over medium-high heat and bring to a simmer. Reduce the heat to medium and skim off any foam that rises to the surface. Simmer until the beef is tender when pierced with a fork, 25 to 30 minutes. Use tongs to transfer the beef to a large bowl to cool. Reserve the broth for another use.

2 Trim off any excess fat from the beef and transfer it to the bowl of a food processor. Pulse until the beef is finely shredded. Transfer the shredded beef to a large bowl and set aside.

3 Thinly slice the remaining onion half and add it to a small bowl with cold water. Set aside.

4 In a small bowl, whisk together the lime juice, serranos, oregano, the remaining 1 teaspoon of

continued

salt, and pepper to taste. Continue whisking and add the olive oil.

5 Drain the onions and add them to the shredded beef. Pour the lime-serrano dressing all over the meat and toss to combine. Let the meat marinate in the dressing for 20 minutes at room temperature. Add the lettuce, radishes, and cilantro and toss to combine. Taste and adjust the seasonings.

6 If using Siete Almond Flour Tortillas, place tortillas on a baking sheet, and bake for 12 minutes, or until golden brown. Let cool. Serve the salpicón on tostadas and garnish with the avocado. Serve immediately at room temperature.

BEEF MILANESA

SERVES 4 | 50 MINUTES | GF, DF

When we were little, we'd join our mom on her weekly grocery store runs. Shopping in a small town meant our mom would stop and chat in almost every aisle with the friends and neighbors we'd run into. But it was all worth it when we'd see her grab thinly cut beef steak and breadcrumbs, because we knew milanesa was on the menu! This meal, breaded and pan-fried until crispy, was one of our dad's favorites—and since we've found a way to make it grain-free, it still is!

1½ pounds beef top round, cut into 4 thin steaks

½ teaspoon fine sea salt, plus more

1 cup warm water

½ cup arrowroot flour

1½ tablespoons flax meal

2 garlic cloves, minced

½ teaspoon freshly ground black pepper

1 cup cassava flour

4 cups Siete Sea Salt Tortilla Chips, or tortilla chips of your choice, blended into very fine crumbs, or 2 cups gluten-free breadcrumbs

Avocado oil, or your favorite oil for frying

Flaky sea salt, for serving

1 Lay the steaks on a piece of parchment paper and season generously with fine sea salt. Set aside.

2 In a wide, shallow bowl, whisk together the warm water, arrowroot flour, flax meal, garlic, pepper, and fine sea salt. Set aside.

3 Add the cassava flour to another wide, shallow bowl. Add the finely blended tortilla chips to a large plate.

4 Dry the steaks thoroughly with a paper towel. Dredge each steak in the cassava flour, followed by the arrowroot mixture, followed by the chip crumbs, firmly pressing the crumbs into the steak. Lay the breaded steak on a piece of parchment paper and cover with another piece of parchment. Repeat with the remaining steaks.

5 In a large cast-iron skillet over medium-high heat, heat about ½ inch of oil to 350°F.

6 Fry each steak for 3 minutes per side, or until golden and crisp. Transfer the cooked steaks to a wire rack set over a baking sheet to drain. Finish with flaky salt and serve.

TACOS DE COLIFLOR

MAKES 4 TO 6 TACOS | 55 MINUTES | GF, DF, V

Tacos have the spectacular ability to bring all of our favorite foods together in a single meal. Barbacoa tacos, chorizo con huevo tacos, crispy tacos, cheese tacos—and now, these cauliflower tacos. We wanted to develop a vegetarian option that was just as flavorful and satisfying as its meat-filled counterparts. With crispy cauliflower, spicy jalapeño crema, and a sprinkle of crunchy cabbage, this veggie taco checks all the boxes!

FOR THE CAULIFLOWER FILLING

1 (2-pound) head of cauliflower, cut into small florets

2 tablespoons fresh lemon juice

½ cup tapioca starch

1 tablespoon nutritional yeast

½ teaspoon sea salt

¼ cup avocado oil

FOR THE TACOS

¼ small head of green cabbage, cored and thinly sliced

1 cup fresh cilantro leaves

1 tablespoon fresh lime juice

¼ teaspoon sea salt

Jalapeño Cashew Crema (page 207)

4 to 6 Siete Grain Free Almond Flour Tortillas, or tortillas of your choice

1 Make the cauliflower filling: In a large bowl, toss the cauliflower with the lemon juice.

2 In a separate small bowl, whisk together the tapioca starch, nutritional yeast, and salt. Add the mixture to the cauliflower and toss to coat.

3 Heat the avocado oil in a large nonstick skillet over low-medium heat. Working in batches, add a single layer of the cauliflower and cook until evenly crispy and golden brown, 5 to 7 minutes. Turn and cook until the other side is golden brown and crisp, a total of 10 to 14 minutes. Transfer the cauliflower to a paper towel–lined plate to drain and repeat with the remaining cauliflower.

4 Make the tacos: In a large bowl, toss together the cabbage, cilantro, lime juice, and salt. Let stand until ready to serve.

5 Wipe down the same large nonstick pan from the cauliflower to remove any leftover crispy cauliflower bits. It's fine to leave any remaining

oil in the pan. Place the pan over medium-high heat and warm the tortillas, one or two at a time, about 30 seconds per side. Transfer the tortillas to a kitchen towel, tortilla basket, or plate tented with foil to keep warm.

6 Drain the cabbage and cilantro mixture.

7 Spread a tablespoon or two of the jalapeño cashew crema on each tortilla. Divide the cauliflower filling among the tortillas and top with the cabbage and cilantro slaw. Serve with additional crema on the side.

QUESADILLAS, AKA "CHEESE TACOS"

MAKES 4 QUESADILLAS | 15 MINUTES | GF, DF [OPTION], V [OPTION]

If our dad had to pick two dishes to eat for the rest of his life, they would be milanesa and quesadillas, which our family lovingly calls "cheese tacos." Quesadillas are easy to make—that's the beauty of the dish. There's nothing more to it than good, melty cheese and fresh tortillas. If you're anything like Bobby, or generally appreciate the simple pleasures in life, this one's for you.

Ghee or avocado oil, for the pan

8 Siete Grain Free Almond Flour Tortillas, or tortillas of your choice

1 cup shredded Oaxaca or quesadilla cheese, or shredded dairy-free cheese

Creamy Avocado Dip (page 203) or Cashew Crema (page 207), for serving

1 In a medium nonstick skillet over medium heat, add a spoonful of ghee or a drizzle of oil.

2 Add a tortilla topped with ¼ cup of the cheese, followed by another tortilla to sandwich the cheese. Cook for 2 to 3 minutes, until the bottom tortilla begins to crisp slightly and the cheese starts to melt. Flip the quesadilla and cook for another 2 minutes, or until the cheese is totally melted. Transfer the quesadilla to a cutting board and cut into 4 wedges. Repeat with the remaining tortillas and cheese.

3 Serve with the avocado dip or cashew crema.

PICADILLO

SERVES 4 TO 6 | 45 MINUTES | GF, DF

On the days we find ourselves standing in front of the fridge with our hands on our hips, trying to figure out what ingredients could possibly come together to make a meal, we make picadillo. It's the ultimate "What do I have right now?" dinner because it doesn't call for more than some ground meat cooked up with whatever vegetables you have on hand. It then becomes a versatile meat-and-veggie base that you can make into pretty much anything—nachos, burritos, bowls, tacos, flautas, tostadas. If you've got picadillo, you've got the beginnings of a delicious dinner!

2 tablespoons avocado or extra-virgin olive oil

1 pound ground beef

Sea salt and freshly ground black pepper

½ pound russet potatoes, peeled and cut into ½-inch cubes

1 medium yellow onion, chopped

2 jalapeño chiles, stemmed, seeded, and minced

3 garlic cloves, chopped

2 teaspoons ground cumin

1 teaspoon ground paprika

½ teaspoon dried Mexican oregano leaves or dried oregano leaves

2 Roma tomatoes, chopped

1¼ cups chicken or beef broth

1 dried bay leaf

¼ cup chopped fresh cilantro, plus more for serving

Mexican Rice (page 134), for serving

Refried Beans (page 131), or store-bought, warmed, for serving

Siete Grain Free Cassava Flour Tortillas, or tortillas of your choice, warmed, for serving

1 Heat the oil in a large, high-sided skillet or Dutch oven over medium-high heat.

2 Add the beef and season with salt and pepper. Cook the beef until just browned, breaking it up with the back of a wooden spoon as it cooks, 7 to 8 minutes. Add the potatoes, onion, jalapeños, garlic, cumin, paprika, oregano, and salt and pepper to taste and cook, stirring frequently, until the onions have softened, about 5 minutes. Stir in the tomatoes, broth, and bay leaf and bring the mixture to a simmer. Reduce the heat to medium-low, cover, and cook for about 10 minutes.

3 Uncover the pan and continue cooking for 10 to 15 more minutes, stirring occasionally, until the potatoes are tender. Remove the pan from the heat, taste, and adjust the seasoning, if needed. Stir in the cilantro and serve with Mexican rice, refried beans, and tortillas.

ARROZ CON POLLO

SERVES 4 TO 6 | 1 HOUR 20 MINUTES | GF, DF

If you ask any of us to pick our favorite dishes from growing up, Grandma Campos's are usually at the top of the list. Atole de galleta, beans, and flour tortillas all come to mind, but the most beloved would have to be her arroz con pollo. It is a true comfort food not only because of its warmth and flavor but also because of its delightful mix of aromas—cumin, tomato, garlic, onion, and chicken. The way they meld together and infuse your kitchen while simmering on the stove is nothing short of mouthwatering.

¼ cup extra-virgin olive oil

2½ teaspoons sea salt

1 teaspoon garlic powder

½ teaspoon ground coriander

½ teaspoon dried Mexican oregano leaves or dried oregano leaves

½ teaspoon ground cumin

Pinch of ground paprika

2½ pounds boneless, skinless chicken thighs

1 large onion, diced

4 garlic cloves, chopped

1½ cups long-grain white rice, thoroughly rinsed and drained

2½ cups chicken broth

¾ cup tomato sauce

1 cup frozen peas and carrots mix, thawed

½ cup chopped fresh cilantro, for serving

2 limes, quartered, for serving

1 In a large bowl, whisk together 3 tablespoons of the olive oil, 1 teaspoon of the salt, the garlic powder, coriander, oregano, cumin, and paprika. Add the chicken and toss to coat. Set aside.

2 Preheat the oven to 350°F.

3 In a large high-sided, oven-safe skillet over medium-high heat, heat the remaining 1 tablespoon of olive oil. Sear the chicken thighs for 3 to 5 minutes per side, until golden and starting to crisp around the edges. Transfer the chicken to a plate and set aside.

4 In the same pan over medium-high heat, add the onion, garlic, and ½ teaspoon of the remaining salt and cook, stirring, until the onion is translucent, 3 to 5 minutes. Stir in the rice and cook until fragrant, about 1 minute. Add the broth, tomato sauce, and the remaining 1 teaspoon of salt and bring the mixture to a boil. Remove the pan from the heat.

5 Nestle the chicken thighs on top of the rice mixture. Cover the pan and carefully transfer it to the oven. Bake for 40 minutes, or until the rice and chicken are cooked through.

6 Transfer the chicken thighs to a plate. Fluff the rice and stir in the peas and carrots. Use a fork to shred the chicken thighs. Add the shredded chicken back to the pan, toss with the rice, and garnish with the cilantro and lime wedges.

FRIJOLIZZAS

MAKES 4 FRIJOLIZZAS | 15 MINUTES | GF

Making dinner for the five of us kids every night was a balancing act. On any given day, some of us would want pizza, some of us would want frijoles, some of us would want tacos. But our mom was up for the challenge. She took two of those cravings and cut what we called *bolillos* (rolls of bread) in half, smeared butter across the top, covered them in frijoles, pizza sauce, and cheese, and then put them in the oven. These resourceful and satisfying creations didn't have a name until one evening when we were having a "smorgasbord night" (what our family called dinners that were constructed entirely out of leftovers and odds and ends from the fridge) our brother Rob asked for "frijolizzas." The name stuck, and so did the recipe.

2 gluten-free rolls of your choice, split

1 tablespoon ghee

½ cup pizza sauce or tomato sauce of your choice

1 cup Refried Beans (page 131), or store-bought, warmed

1 cup shredded cheddar cheese

1 Preheat the broiler to high heat.

2 Heat a broiler-proof nonstick skillet over medium heat. Spread the cut sides of the rolls with the ghee and broil until golden brown, about 3 minutes.

3 Spread 2 tablespoons of the pizza sauce over each piece of bread. Top with a thick layer of refried beans and shredded cheese.

4 Broil for 2 to 3 minutes, until the cheese has completely melted.

LAREDO-STYLE SUSHI

MAKES 4 SUSHI ROLLS | 1 HOUR 15 MINUTES | GF, DF

Just about any type of cuisine can be made using Mexican ingredients—sushi included. Growing up in Laredo, we had few Japanese restaurants, and they all offered their version of "Mexican sushi," a playful twist on the traditional offering with a cream cheese and avocado filling, plus crushed chips, chiles toreados, and chipotle mayo to finish it off. We just wish we'd known that sushi restaurants outside of South Texas don't usually serve sushi with a side of guacamole—a lesson Rob learned the hard way one night in Austin when he popped a large chunk of wasabi in his mouth!

NOTE: This recipe calls for using a sushi mat to help roll the sushi, but no sweat if you don't have one. Alternatively you can use a thick kitchen towel wrapped in plastic wrap to roll your sushi.

1 pound raw shrimp, shelled, deveined, and tails removed

1 tablespoon avocado oil

3 garlic cloves, minced

½ teaspoon sea salt

1 cup sushi rice, rinsed well under cold running water

1 tablespoon rice vinegar

1 teaspoon agave nectar

4 sheets nori seaweed

2 ripe avocados, cut into thin (¼-inch) slices

½ cucumber, peeled, cut into long, thin (¼-inch) strips

4 ounces cream cheese, or dairy-free cream cheese, well-chilled and cut into long, thin (½-inch) pieces

1 (4-ounce) bag Siete Fuego Potato Chips, or spicy potato chips of your choice, crushed

½ cup Chipotle Mayo (page 212)

Chiles Toreados (page 206), for serving

1 In a medium bowl, combine the shrimp, oil, garlic, and ¼ teaspoon of the salt and toss to coat.

2 Heat a large cast-iron or nonstick skillet over medium-high heat. Cook the shrimp for 1 to 2 minutes per side, until just pink. Transfer the shrimp to a cutting board and roughly chop into small chunks. Set aside.

3 In a rice cooker, combine the rice and 1¼ cups of water. Cook using the sushi rice option on your rice cooker.

continued

4 In a small bowl, stir together the rice vinegar, agave nectar, and ¼ teaspoon of salt.

5 Transfer the cooked rice to a medium bowl and season with the vinegar mixture, using a slicing motion throughout the rice to incorporate the seasonings without mashing the rice. Using a turning motion, stir and turn the rice to help it cool.

6 Wrap a sushi mat in a few layers of plastic wrap and seal the edges. Place a sheet of nori over the sushi mat and add about ¼ of the cooked rice over the top. Press the rice to cover the entire sheet of nori in an even layer. Flip the nori so the rice is underneath.

7 Add a few slices of avocado in a horizontal line across the middle of the seaweed. Place shrimp pieces next to the avocado in another horizontal line of similar width. Continue with thinner horizontal lines of the cucumber strips, followed by one strip of the cream cheese. Use the sushi mat to bring the bottom of the nori up over the avocado, and continue rolling, applying gentle pressure, to seal the roll.

8 Roll each sushi roll in the crushed chips. Use a knife dipped in water to cut the roll into 8 pieces. Set aside and repeat with the remaining ingredients to make 4 rolls total.

9 Drizzle each sushi roll with chipotle mayo and serve with the chiles toreados.

5

SIDES/GUARNICIÓNES

What's everyone bringing?" This is the first question that follows the announcement of any family gathering, whether it's a holiday, birthday celebration, or carne asada. When it's time to gather, we all come rolling in with our own contributions—usually an impressive collection of side dishes that we've mastered over the years: a steamy pot of beans, a big container of rice, grilled veggies wrapped in foil, salad in a bowl the size of a wok (and, on a couple of occasions, an actual wok), and a mountain of chips and guac. What's a meal without side dishes, anyway? That way there's always something for everyone, and no matter what the main dish is, there's no shortage of flavors and textures to complement it. It's like we say: "More is more!"

REFRIED BEANS

SERVES 5 | 2.5 HOURS (PLUS 8 HOURS' SOAK TIME) | GF, DF, V

If there's one dish that's on our table at every meal, it's beans—right next to a pan full of rice. Each time we visited Grandma Campos, the aroma of a giant pot of simmering beans would greet us at the door. She liked to use bacon grease or an entire stick of butter as her secret ingredients, but we've found our own special way to make this staple rich and hearty while also being vegan: After cooking the beans in vegetable broth, we sauté them with pickled jalapeños, green bell peppers, and onions in a generous amount of coconut oil. By the time all is said and done, these refried beans deliver the same rich flavor of an abuelita's homemade original!

TIP: One way to make these beans even more nutritious is to sprout them before cooking. After soaking the beans as the recipe calls for, drain and rinse them thoroughly. Put the beans in a large sprouting jar, a 6-cup mason jar, or a container that will allow the beans to double in size. If using a mason jar, replace the metal lid with a layer of cheesecloth and secure it with the metal ring or a rubber band to allow air to circulate into the jar. Keep the container at room temperature and repeat the rinsing and draining 3 to 4 times a day until sprout tails appear. Depending on the ambient temperature of your kitchen, sprouting can take anywhere from 2 to 4 days. Rinse one final time and drain the beans thoroughly before cooking.

2 cups dried pinto beans

4 cups vegetable broth

1½ teaspoons sea salt

2 tablespoons avocado oil

½ yellow onion, finely diced, plus more for serving

1 green bell pepper, stemmed, seeded, and finely diced

¼ cup pickled jalapeños, drained and finely diced, plus more to taste

¼ cup fresh cilantro leaves, chopped, for serving

1 In a colander, rinse the beans and remove any stones or loose debris. In a medium bowl, combine the beans and 4 cups of water. Soak for at least 8 hours or overnight, drain, and rinse.

continued

2 In a large pot over medium-high heat, add the beans and vegetable broth. Bring to a boil and add 1 teaspoon of the salt. Reduce the heat to a simmer, cover, and cook until the beans are soft and the skins are no longer tough or squeaky, 1 to 1½ hours.

3 Transfer the beans and half of their broth to a blender. Reserve the remaining broth. Blend the beans into a smooth paste.

4 Add the oil in a large, high-sided skillet over medium heat. Add the onion and bell pepper and cook until the vegetables are soft and golden brown around the edges, 8 to 10 minutes. Stir in the pickled jalapeños and the remaining ½ teaspoon of salt.

5 Add the pureed beans to the pan, mashing them lightly into the vegetable mixture. Reduce the heat to a simmer, cover, and cook, occasionally mashing the beans and vegetables lightly and adding some of the reserved broth to reach the desired texture. Cook until the refried beans are creamy, about 45 minutes. Taste and adjust the seasoning with more salt, if needed.

6 To serve, ladle the beans with some of their broth into bowls and garnish with the onion and cilantro.

MEXICAN RICE

SERVES 4 | 45 MINUTES | GF, DF, V

Mexican rice is one of those traditional dishes that's celebrated whenever it's at our table. Even though it's usually served with its trusty sidekick of refried beans, this rice is a strong enough side to stand on its own thanks to the robust flavor from cilantro, jalapeño, and tomatoes.

1½ cups long-grain white rice,
such as jasmine or basmati

2 cups chopped Roma tomatoes

2 cups vegetable broth or water

½ cup chopped yellow onion

1 tablespoon tomato paste

1 tablespoon sea salt

¼ cup avocado oil

4 garlic cloves, minced

¼ cup chopped fresh cilantro leaves (optional)

Freshly ground black pepper

1 dried bay leaf

1 jalapeño, stemmed, halved lengthwise,
and seeded, for serving

1 Rinse the rice until the water drains almost completely clear, 5 to 7 times. Transfer the rice to a colander to drain well.

2 In a blender, combine the tomatoes, broth, onions, tomato paste, and salt. Blend until smooth.

3 In a large nonstick skillet with a tight-fitting lid over medium-low heat, add 3 tablespoons of the avocado oil and the garlic. Cook, stirring frequently, until the garlic is aromatic, about 2 minutes. Add the rice and cook until the grains start to turn opaque and begin to smell nutty, about 5 minutes. Stir in the tomato mixture, cilantro, and black pepper to taste and increase the heat to medium-high. Bring the rice mixture to a boil and add the bay leaf. Cover and reduce the heat to low. Cook the rice undisturbed for 20 to 23 minutes, until tender. Remove the pan from the heat, leaving the lid on to let the rice rest for another 5 minutes.

4 Remove the lid and gently fluff the rice with a fork, combining any tomato pulp left on the top. Drizzle the remaining 1 tablespoon of avocado oil over the rice and let it rest for 5 more minutes before serving. Divide the rice among plates and garnish with the jalapeño.

MEXICAN CAULIFLOWER RICE

SERVES 4 | 30 MINUTES | GF, DF, V

When our family decided to give up grains, one of the hardest foods to say goodbye to—next to tortillas—was rice. It is, after all, a hugely popular Mexican side dish. So you can imagine how excited we were to discover that you can treat riced cauliflower exactly as you would rice and end up with a grain-free substitute that's equally flavorful, satisfying, and versatile.

NOTE: If you'd still like to include traditional rice in your rotation but want an easy way to get in a serving of veggies, substitute half of your rice with this cauliflower alternative.

½ medium head of cauliflower, broken into bite-sized florets

3 tablespoons avocado oil

4 garlic cloves, finely minced

¼ cup tomato paste

2 teaspoons onion powder

1½ teaspoons sea salt

½ cup coarsely chopped fresh cilantro leaves

1 In a food processor, add about half of the cauliflower and pulse until the pieces are about the size of a grain of rice, about 10 pulses. Transfer the riced cauliflower to a medium bowl and repeat with the remaining cauliflower florets.

2 In a large skillet over medium-low heat, heat 1 tablespoon of the oil. Add the garlic and cook, stirring frequently, until fragrant, about 2 minutes. Whisk in ⅓ cup of water, plus the tomato paste, onion powder, and ½ teaspoon of the salt. Cook until the sauce has thickened slightly, about 2 minutes. Transfer the sauce to a small bowl and return the skillet to the heat.

3 Heat the remaining 2 tablespoons of oil in the skillet and increase the heat to medium. Add the cauliflower and the remaining 1 teaspoon of salt and stir to combine. Cover and cook, stirring occasionally, until the cauliflower is tender, about 5 minutes. Pour the tomato sauce over the cauliflower, increase the heat to high, and stir to coat the cauliflower in the sauce. Continue stirring and cook until most of the moisture has evaporated, 2 to 4 more minutes.

4 Remove the pan from the heat and toss in the cilantro. Fluff the cauliflower rice with a fork and serve.

POBLANO RICE

SERVES 4 | 45 MINUTES | GF, DF, V [OPTION]

Poblano rice, *arroz verde*, or "green rice"—whichever name you know it by, there's no denying the inclusion of this dish in many Mexican restaurants. The rice in this dish gets cooked in a base broth made from poblanos, onions, and fresh cilantro, and is perfect for serving alongside seafood and enchiladas, as the base of burrito bowls, and—of course—with beans.

1½ cups long-grain white rice,
such as jasmine or basmati

3 poblano chiles

1½ cups chicken or vegetable broth

¼ cup chopped yellow onion

1½ teaspoons sea salt, plus more if needed

3 tablespoons avocado oil

2 garlic cloves, chopped

¼ cup chopped fresh cilantro leaves

Lime wedges, for serving

1 Rinse the rice until the water drains almost completely clear, 5 to 7 times. Transfer the rice to a colander to drain well.

2 Using tongs, char the poblanos directly on the stovetop over high heat until blackened in spots, about 5 minutes per side. (Alternatively, you can lightly coat the peppers with cooking spray, arrange them on a baking sheet, and roast at 425°F until the peppers have darkened on all sides, about 30 minutes.) Transfer the charred poblanos to a bowl and cover immediately with a plate to create steam and loosen up the tough skins. Let the poblanos sit and steam for 10 minutes. When cool enough to handle, rub your fingers over the poblanos to peel off as much skin as possible. Discard the skins, stems, and seeds. Set aside 2 of the whole poblanos and finely dice the remaining poblano.

3 In a blender, combine the 2 whole poblanos, the broth, onion, and salt and blend until smooth. Set aside.

4 In a large nonstick skillet with a tight-fitting lid, heat the oil over low heat. Add the garlic and cook, stirring frequently until fragrant, about 2 minutes. Increase the heat to medium, add the rice, and cook until the grains start to turn opaque and begin to smell nutty, stirring occasionally, about 5 minutes. Add the pureed poblano mixture. Stir gently to combine and bring to a simmer. Cover the pan with the lid, reduce the heat to low, and cook the rice undisturbed for 13 to 15 minutes, until tender.

5 Remove the pan from the heat and add the diced poblanos and cilantro, but do not stir. Replace the lid and let the rice rest for another 10 minutes. Remove the lid and gently fluff the rice with a fork, mixing the diced poblano and cilantro into the rice. Taste and adjust the seasoning with more salt, if needed.

6 Serve warm with lime wedges.

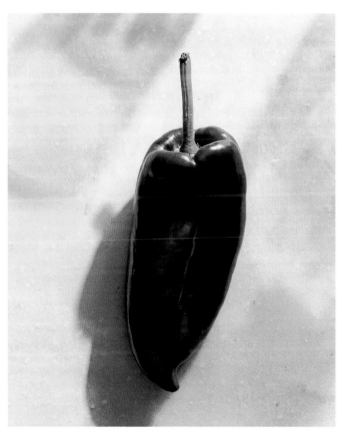

NOPALITO SALAD

SERVES 4 | 15 MINUTES (PLUS 1 HOUR FOR SALTING) | GF, DF, V

This light, refreshing side dish is our updated version of Grandma Campos's fried *nopales*, or cactus paddles. It's a great way to add a little green to your plate. In fact, you could even say that it makes a fan-cactus addition to any meal. If you can't find fresh nopales paddles, you can use canned or jarred nopales; just skip the cooking steps and go straight to assembling the salad.

NOTE: To keep your nopales a nice, bright green color, try the salting method: Place your nopales paddles on a baking sheet lined with paper towels. Sprinkle 1 teaspoon of salt on each side of the paddles, a total of 2 teaspoons of salt per nopal. Set aside until the nopales have released some of their moisture and slime, 45 minutes to 1 hour. Once the nopales have released moisture and liquid has accumulated around them, rub the salt against the nopales with your fingers. Place them under running water to rinse off excess salt. Pat dry with a kitchen towel and finely dice the nopales. Proceed with the rest of the recipe.

———

1 tablespoon avocado oil

2 nopales paddles, thorns removed, or 8 ounces cactus in brine, drained and rinsed

½ teaspoon sea salt, plus more if needed

½ small red onion, finely chopped

½ pound Roma tomatoes, seeded and finely chopped

¼ cup fresh lime juice

⅓ cup finely chopped fresh cilantro leaves

1 avocado, halved, pitted, and cut into 1-inch half-moons

1 jalapeño chile, stemmed, seeded, and finely minced

1 Preheat a grill for direct, medium heat, or a grill pan over medium-high heat.

2 If using fresh nopales, drizzle or brush the oil onto the nopales and season with the salt. If using canned or jarred cactus in brine, drain, rinse well to remove the brine, dry well, and omit the salt. Skip the cooking step below.

3 Grill the nopales until grill marks develop, about 5 minutes. Flip and grill until slightly charred, about 5 more minutes. Season with more salt as needed. Transfer the grilled nopales to a cutting board and finely dice.

4 Rinse the onion under cold water to remove some of its sharp bite. Drain and dry the onion thoroughly.

5 In a medium bowl, combine the nopales, onion, tomatoes, lime juice, cilantro, avocado, and jalapeño. Give this a gentle stir to combine and serve immediately.

CHARRO BEANS

SERVES 4-6 | 2 HOURS (PLUS 8 HOURS' SOAK TIME) | GF, DF

Charro beans, in contrast to smooth, creamy refried beans, can be described as "bean soup." Always served in a bowl on the side, these beans usually have sausage, bacon, onions, tomatoes, and cilantro tossed in. Our family likes to enjoy beans the way we like to enjoy conversations around the table: in good, hearty company. The result is savory, brothy, soupy goodness.

2 cups dried pinto beans

4 cups chicken broth

2 large jalapeños

1¾ teaspoons sea salt

2 ounces bacon, chopped

4 ounces smoked sausage, finely diced

½ medium yellow onion, finely chopped

1 tablespoon tomato paste

1 pound Roma tomatoes, finely diced

½ cup finely chopped fresh cilantro leaves and stems

1 In a colander, rinse the beans and remove any stones or loose debris. In a medium bowl, combine the beans and 4 cups of water. Soak for at least 8 hours or overnight, drain, and rinse.

2 In a large pot over medium-high heat, add the beans, 2 cups of the chicken broth, jalapeños, and 2 cups of water. Bring to a boil and add 1 teaspoon of the salt. Reduce the heat to a simmer, cover, and cook until the beans are tender but slightly firm, 30 to 40 minutes. Season with another ½ teaspoon of the salt.

3 In a Dutch oven or large heavy-bottomed pot over medium heat, add the bacon. Cook until the fat is rendered and the bacon is crispy, 6 to 8 minutes. Transfer the bacon with a slotted spoon to a plate lined with a paper towel to drain.

4 Add the smoked sausage in the remaining rendered fat and fry gently until slightly crispy, about 5 minutes. Transfer to the plate with the bacon.

5 Add the onions and tomato paste to the rendered fat and cook until the onions are translucent, about 5 minutes. Add the tomatoes, cilantro, and remaining ¼ teaspoon of salt and cook, stirring, for 5 more minutes. Add the beans, plus the bacon, sausage, and the remaining 2 cups of chicken broth. Cook until the beans are creamy and tender and the vegetables have broken down into a slightly thick, brothy consistency, about 45 minutes.

ROASTED SWEET POTATOES
with PILONCILLO and BUTTER

SERVES 4 | 1 HOUR | GF, DF [OPTION], V [OPTION]

Crispy papas, flautas de papas, papitas preparadas—we've never met a potato dish we didn't like. Here, sweet potatoes are slathered in vegan butter or ghee, then roasted until tender and creamy and given a caramelized *piloncillo* (Mexican brown sugar) crust. These make a great addition to carne asadas or barbecues, especially when roasted above the coals of the fire. Serve them as a side or as a simple but decadently flavorful dessert.

NOTE: Sweet potatoes work well on the grill too, especially if already using it to cook your main. Just place the foil-wrapped sweet potatoes directly on the coals of a charcoal grill heated to medium heat and cook until very tender, about 1 hour. The sweet potatoes will take on a subtle smoky flavor.

---

4 sweet potatoes, scrubbed and thoroughly dried

2 teaspoons vegan butter or ghee, plus more for serving

2 teaspoons fine sea salt

1 small (1-ounce) cone piloncillo

Flaky sea salt, for finishing

1 Preheat the oven to 425°F.

2 Prick the sweet potatoes all over with a knife or fork and rub each sweet potato with the vegan butter or ghee. Sprinkle the fine sea salt all over the sweet potatoes and wrap each sweet potato in a double layer of foil. Set the wrapped potatoes on a baking sheet and roast for about 45 minutes, until easily pierced with a fork.

3 Turn off the oven and turn on the broiler. Carefully unwrap the hot sweet potatoes and return them to the baking sheet. Broil the potatoes, watching carefully, until they're a bit charred on one side, 3 to 5 minutes. Flip the sweet potatoes and repeat to char on the other side.

4 Using a sharp paring knife, carefully cut a slit in each sweet potato. Generously top the potatoes with more butter, then grate the piloncillo on top using a box grater. Finish with flaky salt and serve.

GRILLED CARROTS
with MOLE and CREMA

SERVES 4 TO 6 | 35 MINUTES | GF, DF, V

If there's anything better than carrots grilled over a mesquite fire until charred and caramelized, it's those same grilled carrots served with a deliciously rich mole sauce. (We believe mole over anything is a recipe for success!) If it's not grilling season where you live, you can achieve a similar charred result by cooking the carrots in a cast-iron skillet.

NOTE: Mole almendrado is great with enchiladas—substitute the tomatillo salsa verde in Enchiladas Verdes (page 96) with the mole almendrado and sprinkle with some sesame seeds in place of the sliced onion.

1 tablespoon avocado oil

2 teaspoons fresh lemon juice

½ teaspoon sea salt, plus more to taste

2 pounds carrots, peeled, trimmed, and halved lengthwise

1 teaspoon finely chopped fresh parsley leaves

1 to 1½ cups Mole Almendrado (page 107)

½ cup Cashew Crema (page 207), for serving

2 tablespoons toasted sesame seeds, for serving

1 Preheat a grill or large cast-iron skillet over medium-high heat.

2 In a large bowl, whisk together the oil, lemon juice, and salt. Add the carrots to the dressing and toss to coat.

3 Lay the carrots on the grill or in the pan, covered, flipping every 10 minutes, or as needed to prevent burning. When flipping the carrots, brush them with more of the seasoned olive oil. Continue cooking until nice grill marks develop and the carrots are fork-tender, about 20 minutes.

4 On a large platter, spread the mole almendrado. Place the carrots on top, drizzle with the cashew crema, and sprinkle with the sesame seeds.

JICAMA, MANGO, AND BLACK SESAME SLAW

SERVES 8 | 20 MINUTES | GF, DF, V

Coming up with this dish was a true "eureka!" moment for us—or perhaps more like a "jicama!" moment. The secret to this refreshing, crunchy slaw is really in the sauce, a tangy blend of chile-lime seasoning and lime juice. These days there's rarely a cookout that goes by without this new citrusy salad on the table.

2 cups jicama cut into 2-inch matchsticks

4 cups mango cut into 2-inch matchsticks

½ head red cabbage, cored and thinly sliced

1 cup Chamoy (page 209), or store-bought

¼ cup Chile-Lime Seasoning (page 210), or store-bought

Juice of 3 limes

1 tablespoon black sesame seeds

In a large bowl, combine the jicama, mango, cabbage, chamoy, chile-lime seasoning, and lime juice and toss thoroughly to coat. Sprinkle with the sesame seeds and mix once again. Keep refrigerated until ready to serve.

MEXICAN CHOPPED SALAD

SERVES 6 | 35 MINUTES | GF, DF, V

At Siete, we do our best to have what we call a "family meal" every Friday, where we can get together and kick our feet up after the working week. This recipe is frequently on rotation at these gatherings because it's an easy way to feed a bunch of hungry people and, like a good salad should, it has layers of flavor from a wide variety of mix-ins like black beans, charred corn, fresh peppers, and tomatillos. It's the kind of dish that ensures the perfect bite every time! This recipe can easily be scaled up if you're expecting a crowd or bringing this to a picnic, potluck, or barbecue.

FOR THE DRESSING

½ avocado

¾ cup fresh lime juice

¼ cup chopped white onion

3 tablespoons chopped fresh cilantro

2 tablespoons chopped pickled jalapeño, from Escabeche (page 215), or store-bought

1 tablespoon coconut sugar

1 teaspoon garlic powder

1 teaspoon sea salt

½ teaspoon dried Mexican oregano leaves or dried oregano leaves

1 cup avocado oil

FOR THE SALAD

1 tablespoon avocado or extra-virgin olive oil

1 cup corn kernels, fresh or frozen and thawed

Sea salt

1 large head of romaine lettuce, finely chopped

1 cup cooked or canned black beans

2 Persian cucumbers, finely diced

1 Roma tomato, finely diced

1 sweet orange or red bell pepper, stemmed, seeded, and finely diced

½ cup finely diced red onion

¼ cup chopped fresh cilantro

1 avocado, cut into ½-inch pieces

3 medium tomatillos, husked, rinsed, and thinly sliced

1 **Make the dressing:** In a high-speed blender, add the avocado, lime juice, onion, cilantro, pickled jalapeño, coconut sugar, garlic powder, salt, oregano, and ½ cup of water and blend until smooth. With the blender running, slowly stream in the oil and blend for 30 more seconds. Set aside.

2 In a large cast-iron skillet or nonstick sauté pan over medium-high heat, heat the oil. Add the corn and season with salt. Cook, stirring occasionally, until the corn is charred on a few sides, about 7 minutes. Remove the pan from the heat.

3 **Make the salad:** In a large bowl, add the chopped lettuce, black beans, cucumbers, tomato, bell pepper, onion, cilantro, charred corn kernels, and about 1 cup of the dressing. Toss thoroughly to combine. Add more dressing and salt and toss again. Add the avocado and tomatillos and gently toss once more. Serve with the remaining dressing on the side.

6

DESSERTS/POSTRES

Growing up, desserts and sweets were special treats to be enjoyed on particularly celebratory occasions—at weddings, on birthdays, and during the holidays. But while there was unparalleled excitement around enjoying a piece of tres leches cake after singing "Happy Birthday" or dunking freshly made, melt-in-your-mouth buñuelos into cajeta on Christmas, it was the small moments in between that were sometimes the sweetest. Slurping icy paletas in the summertime, devouring a bag of freshly baked apple empanadas on a lazy Sunday morning, snacking on the mazapan that our parents let us pick from the glass displays at local restaurants—these were the simple pleasures that marked many precious memories.

In this chapter you'll find recipes for occasions large and small, extra-special and everyday. From sweets to start your day, to after-dinner treats, to once-a-year novelties, we think you'll find that we've left no indulgence behind.

PALETAS

Paletas, or popsicles, are synonymous with hot Texas summers. When we were little, we would visit our grandparents in Houston. They didn't have a swimming pool, so Grandpa would bring each of us individual ice chests and fill them with water from the hose for us to sit in while we slurped on paletas, trying to stay cool.

Paletas come in a variety of flavors, from tropical fruits to almond to horchata. Two of our favorites, which are considered classic Mexican flavors, are mangonada and tamarindo. Mangonada is the epitome of bright and refreshing thanks to the trifecta of mango, chamoy, and chile-lime seasoning. Tamarindo gets its sweet-and-sour flavor from its namesake pod-like fruit, tamarind, which requires boiling before it can be pureed and frozen, but after a taste on a hot summer day, you'll know the effort was well worth it.

MANGONADA PALETAS

MAKES 6 POPSICLES | 30 MINUTES (PLUS 4 HOURS FOR FREEZING) | GF, DF, V

1½ cups frozen mango chunks

1 cup fresh orange juice

Juice of 1 lime

¼ cup Chamoy (page 209), or store-bought

Chile-Lime Seasoning (page 210), or store-bought for serving

1 In a high-speed blender, combine the mango chunks, orange juice, and lime juice and blend until completely smooth.

2 Using a small spoon, drip a few teaspoons of chamoy down the insides of 6 ice pop molds.

3 Divide the mango mixture among the molds and let the chamoy and mango mix to create a marble pattern. Insert ice pop sticks into the middle of each mold and freeze until completely solid, at least 4 hours. To release the paletas from their molds, run the molds briefly under warm water.

4 To serve, remove the paletas from the molds and sprinkle each with chile-lime seasoning to taste.

TAMARINDO PALETAS

MAKES 8 POPSICLES | 30 MINUTES (PLUS 4 HOURS FOR FREEZING) | GF, DF, V

7 -ounces tamarind pods, or 5 ounces tamarind pulp or paste

⅓ cup maple syrup

2 teaspoons fresh lemon juice

1 teaspoon vanilla extract

1 Remove the hard shells from the tamarind pods and discard the roots and strings attached to the flesh.

2 In a medium saucepan over medium heat, combine the tamarind pods (or pulp, if using) with 3 cups of water. Bring to a boil, then reduce the heat to a gentle simmer. Cook, mashing the pods occasionally with a potato masher until the tamarind is tender, for 20 minutes. Remove the pan from the heat, cover, and let the tamarind soak for 10 more minutes. Carefully transfer the tamarind and cooking liquid to a medium bowl and let cool completely. Set the pan aside, but don't rinse it.

3 Strain the tamarind and cooking liquid through a fine-mesh sieve into a medium bowl. Press the pulp through the sieve and discard the seeds and any remaining strings or shells.

4 Transfer the mixture to a spouted measuring cup and measure 1½ cups, adding more water to make up the balance if needed. Stir in the maple syrup, lemon juice, and vanilla.

5 Divide the mixture among 8 ice pop molds and insert the sticks. Freeze for at least 4 hours or up to overnight. To release the paletas from their molds, run them briefly under warm water.

VEGAN CHURROS

MAKES 12 (3-INCH) CHURROS | 1.5 HOURS | GF, DF, V

This recipe transports us to restaurants in our hometown, where you could order a plate full of churros with large containers of cajeta and chocolate for dunking. It also reminds us of childhood days when we'd visit local fairs and carnivals. We'd walk around, paper-wrapped churro in hand, the cinnamon and sugar sticking to our fingers, as we caught up with friends and waited in line for rides.

Our vegan version of this classic confection swaps out butter and eggs for coconut shortening and psyllium husk powder, which will give you the same signature soft interior and crispy, caramelized exterior.

NOTE: You'll notice that this recipe calls for coconut shortening. Don't be tempted to use coconut oil instead! The two are not interchangeable in this preparation.

FOR THE CINNAMON SUGAR

¼ cup coconut sugar

1 tablespoon ground cinnamon

Pinch of sea salt

FOR THE CHURROS

½ cup coconut shortening

1 teaspoon coconut sugar

½ teaspoon sea salt

1 cup white rice flour plus 1 tablespoon potato flour

½ teaspoon psyllium husk powder

Avocado oil, or your favorite oil for frying

1 **Make the cinnamon sugar:** In a small bowl, combine the coconut sugar, cinnamon, and salt and set aside.

2 **Make the churros:** In a small saucepan over medium heat, add the shortening, coconut sugar, salt, and 1 cup of water and heat, stirring occasionally, until the shortening is melted. Reduce the heat to low and sprinkle in the flour mixture. Stir with a spatula or wooden spoon, working quickly, as the dough will immediately start to thicken. Mix until a dough forms and most of the lumps smooth out, about 1 minute. The dough

continued

should be a fairly uniform ball, and the bottom of the dough should stick slightly to the pot.

3 In a blender, add ½ cup of water and the psyllium husk powder and blend until smooth. Let the mixture rest until it thickens, about 10 minutes.

4 Transfer the dough to a stand mixer fitted with the whisk attachment. Add the psyllium mixture and beat on medium speed for 1 to 2 minutes, until the mixture is glossy and well combined.

5 Line a baking sheet with parchment paper. Transfer the dough mixture to a double-layered plastic piping bag (or a single cloth piping bag) fitted with a star tip.

6 Using a large star tip, pipe the mixture in 3-inch lengths onto the parchment. (Alternatively, churros can be piped into long lines, then cut into 3-inch lengths with scissors after frying.) The mixture may take some effort to pipe out, and it is normal to see some oil separating from the dough.

7 In a large, high-sided skillet over medium-high heat, heat about 1 to 2 inches of oil to 375°F.

8 Working in batches, carefully add a few churros to the hot oil and fry for 1 to 2 minutes, until golden brown and crispy. Drain the churros on a wire rack set over a baking sheet. Toss the churros in the cinnamon sugar while still warm and serve immediately.

PECAN BROWNIES
WITH COCONUT CAJETA

SERVES 9 | 1.5 HOURS | GF, DF, V

When our mom was little, Grandma Campos reserved special "jobs" for her and her siblings as ways for them to feel helpful and included in the kitchen. Some of this was due—in part—to only trusting them with tasks that didn't impact the outcome of a meal or prolong the process, like chopping up the vegetables or mixing the batter when baking. This is not only the perfect recipe for letting small hands help, it's also a delicious Mexican twist on a gooey, chocolate-y classic that just so happens to be gluten-free.

¾ cup melted coconut oil, plus more for the pan

2 tablespoons flax meal

1½ cups almond flour

1¼ cups coconut sugar

½ cup tapioca flour

½ cup unsweetened Dutch-process cocoa powder

¼ cup chickpea flour

1 teaspoon baking powder

¼ teaspoon sea salt

¾ cup semisweet chocolate chips

1 cup raw unsalted pecans, coarsely chopped

2 tablespoons Coconut Cajeta (page 161), plus more for serving

Flaky sea salt, for finishing

1 Preheat the oven to 325°F. Lightly grease an 8 x 8-inch baking dish with coconut oil and set aside.

2 In a small bowl, whisk together the flax meal and ¼ cup of water. Set aside for 5 minutes to thicken.

3 In a medium bowl, whisk together the almond flour, coconut sugar, tapioca flour, cocoa powder, chickpea flour, baking powder, and salt. Add the melted coconut oil, plus the flax meal mixture, and stir to combine. Gently fold in the chocolate chips. Add the batter to the prepared baking dish and use a spatula to even the top.

4 In a small bowl, toss the chopped pecans with the coconut cajeta. Spread the pecan mixture over the brownie batter, lightly pressing it in.

continued

5 Bake until the edges are slightly firm and dry and a toothpick inserted into the center comes out clean, 25 to 30 minutes.

6 Let the brownies cool in the pan for at least 20 to 30 minutes, or ideally overnight, to com- pletely set and firm up. Cut the brownies into 9 squares. Arrange the brownies on a platter and serve with additional cajeta and flaky salt. Store leftover brownies in an airtight container in the refrigerator for up to 1 week.

COCONUT CAJETA

MAKES ABOUT 2 CUPS | 20 MINUTES | GF, DF, V

This thick, sweet milk caramel is perfectly suited for drizzling over ice cream, dunking buñuelos and churros, or enjoying straight out of the container. Traditional cajeta is made with goat's milk, but we've created a dairy-free version that's every bit as rich and decadent as the original.

⅔ cup full-fat coconut milk

⅔ cup maple syrup

½ cup powdered sugar

¼ cup coconut sugar

2 tablespoons unsweetened cashew butter

2 teaspoons fresh lemon juice

Pinch of sea salt

1 In a blender, add the coconut milk, maple syrup, powdered sugar, coconut sugar, ca- shew butter, lemon juice, and salt and blend until completely smooth.

2 Transfer the mixture to a medium sauce- pan over medium heat. Bring to a simmer and reduce the heat to low. Cook, stirring, for about 5 minutes, until the cajeta thickens and becomes a dark caramel color. Store the cajeta in a sealed jar in the refrigerator for up to 2 weeks.

ALMOND MAZAPAN

MAKES 8 TO 10 MAZAPANS (DEPENDING ON THE SIZE OF YOUR MOLDS) | 30 MINUTES | GF, DF, V [OPTION]

"3, 2, 1 . . . go!" Then the mazapan competition began. We'd be huddled around the table, mazapan in hand, waiting to see who could unwrap theirs the quickest. But here's the tricky part: To win, you could not break it! And if there's one thing we know about eating *mazapan*—a confection traditionally made with ground nuts and sugar—it's that to open it without it crumbling is a true skill. While our family's recipe has always called for peanuts (it can vary from region to region), we've updated things slightly by swapping in creamy cashew butter for an even richer texture.

2 cups powdered sugar

1 cup raw unsalted almonds

⅔ cup unsweetened cashew butter

1 teaspoon sea salt

1 In a food processor, combine the powdered sugar, almonds, cashew butter, and salt and process for 2 to 3 minutes, stopping occasionally to scrape down the sides of the bowl. The nut mixture will become crumbly and start to build on itself and work up the sides of the bowl, then fall back down. Continue to blend until the mixture is uniform and will stay together when pressed.

2 Place a round cookie cutter or ring mold on a piece of parchment paper. Spoon a few heaping tablespoons of the nut mixture into the mold. Starting from the sides and working your way toward the center, use the back of the spoon to press down and smooth the surface of the mixture, turning the parchment as you go. To unmold, gently hold the mazapan down with your fingers while you lift the mold off. Gently flip the mazapan onto a plate and repeat with the remaining nut mixture.

3 Serve immediately or store the mazapan in single layers on parchment paper in an airtight container for up to 1 week.

APPLE EMPANADAS

MAKES 12 EMPANADAS | 2 HOURS | GF, DF, V

On weekends, when our mom didn't make her special Sunday-morning spread for us, our parents and grandparents would leave the house in the early hours to buy breakfast instead. Upon their return, the smell of the still-warm goods coaxed us out of our beds. There were always tacos, along with a bag of mixed pan dulce, which included apple empanadas. To bite into one of these was like eating a warm slice of apple pie, which, thanks to this recipe, you can now re-create grain-free!

NOTE: Because this is a grain-free dough, it will be delicate to work with and tearing is normal. If your dough does tear while shaping the empanadas, you can just patch it back together.

FOR THE FILLING

2 large Honeycrisp apples, peeled, cored, and diced

¼ cup maple syrup

1 teaspoon ground cinnamon

¼ teaspoon freshly grated nutmeg

1 whole clove

Pinch of sea salt

FOR THE DOUGH AND FINISHING

2 cups almond flour

1¼ cups cassava flour, plus more for dusting

½ cup tapioca flour

1 teaspoon sea salt

Avocado oil, or your favorite oil for frying

Coconut sugar, for dusting

1 **Make the filling:** In a medium saucepan over medium heat, add the apples, maple syrup, cinnamon, nutmeg, clove, and salt and stir to combine. Cook, stirring, for about 5 minutes, until the mixture begins to simmer. Reduce the heat to medium-low to maintain a healthy simmer. Cook, stirring occasionally, for about 15 minutes, until the apples are very soft but retain some of their shape. Remove the pan from the heat and let the apple mixture cool completely. Remove and discard the clove.

continued

2 Make the dough: In a medium bowl, whisk together the almond flour, cassava flour, tapioca flour, and salt. Add 1 cup of water and stir to combine. Use your hands if needed to help the dough fully come together.

3 Assemble and fry the empanadas: Divide the dough into 12 equal pieces and shape each piece into a ball. Dust the plastic sheets of a tortilla press with cassava flour and press each dough ball into a round. If you do not have a tortilla press, cut two sections of parchment paper into large enough squares to press the dough, about 7 inches by 7 inches wide. Dust the sheets with cassava flour and place a dough ball onto one piece of floured parchment. Cover the dough with another layer of parchment and roll each dough ball into a flat circle using a rolling pin. Repeat with each of the remaining dough balls.

4 Place a few tablespoons of the cooled apple filling in the center of each round. Use your fingers to fold the dough over the filling and press the edges down to seal. If you find your dough doesn't want to seal, wet your finger and dampen the outer edges of the dough before pressing and sealing. Crimp the edges of each empanada with the tines of a fork or decorative twists, if you like.

5 In a large cast-iron skillet over medium-high heat, heat about 3 inches of oil to 350°F.

6 Fry each empanada for about 2 minutes per side, until golden and crisp. Transfer the hot empanadas to a cooling rack set over a baking sheet and dust generously with coconut sugar. Repeat with the remaining empanadas and serve warm.

PECAN PIE EMPANADAS

MAKES 12 EMPANADAS | 1.5 HOURS | GF, DF, V

In Texas, where you can find pecan trees pretty much everywhere, pecan pie reigns supreme. While we rarely make a whole pie outside of holidays and other special gatherings, this handheld version of the beloved Texan dessert is a fun way to parcel up those same flavors. Enjoy these empanadas for breakfast, or as a dessert topped with a scoop of dairy-free vanilla ice cream.

NOTE: Because this is a grain-free dough, it will be delicate to work with and tearing is normal. If your dough does tear while shaping the empanadas, you can just patch it back together.

FOR THE FILLING

1½ cups finely chopped pecans

¾ cup coconut sugar

3 tablespoons arrowroot flour

½ teaspoon sea salt

3 tablespoons coconut oil, melted

1½ teaspoons vanilla extract

FOR THE DOUGH AND FINISHING

2 cups almond flour

1¼ cups cassava flour, plus more for dusting

½ cup tapioca flour

1 teaspoon sea salt

Avocado oil, or your favorite oil for frying

Coconut sugar, for dusting

1 **Make the filling:** In a medium bowl, toss together the pecans, coconut sugar, arrowroot, and salt. Add the melted coconut oil and vanilla and stir to combine. It will be a crumbly mixture.

2 **Make the dough:** In a medium bowl, whisk together the almond flour, cassava flour, tapioca flour, and salt. Add 1 cup of water and stir to combine. Use your hands if needed to help the dough fully come together.

3 **Assemble and fry the empanadas:** Divide the dough into 12 equal pieces and shape each piece into a ball. Dust the plastic sheets of a tortilla press with cassava flour and press each dough ball into a round. If you do not have a tortilla press, cut two sections of parchment paper into large enough squares to press the dough, about 7 inches by 7 inches wide. Dust the sheets with cassava flour and place a dough ball onto one piece of floured parchment. Cover the dough with another layer

continued

of parchment and roll each dough ball into a flat circle using a rolling pin. Repeat with each of the remaining dough balls.

4 Place about 2 tablespoons of the pecan filling in the center of each round. Use your fingers to fold the dough over the filling and press the edges down to seal. If you find your dough doesn't want to seal, wet your finger and dampen the outer edges of the dough before pressing and sealing. Crimp the edges of each empanada with the tines of a fork or decorative twists, if you like.

5 In a large cast-iron skillet over medium-high heat, heat about 3 inches of oil to 350°F.

6 Fry each empanada for about 2 minutes per side, until golden and crisp. Transfer the hot empanadas to a cooling rack set over a baking sheet to drain and dust generously with coconut sugar. Repeat with the remaining empanadas and serve warm.

FLAN WITH PILONCILLO CARAMEL

SERVES 6 | 20 MINUTES (PLUS 6 HOURS FOR CHILLING) | GF, DF, V

Not sure what to make for dessert? Torn between cake, custard, caramel, and dulce de leche? Look no further than this dairy-free flan, which combines the best of all of these sweets into one silky, custardy, and delightfully jiggly offering. Flan can be made with a variety of flavorings—such as coffee, orange, vanilla, pineapple, cream cheese, and chocolate—but we're partial to this version with *piloncillo* (Mexican brown sugar) and caramel.

4 ounces piloncillo, broken up with a mortar and pestle or meat tenderizer

1½ cups unsweetened cashew milk

1½ cups full-fat canned unsweetened coconut milk

¼ cup coconut sugar

2 teaspoons vanilla extract

1 teaspoon chickpea flour

1 teaspoon tapioca flour

½ teaspoon agar agar

½ teaspoon sea salt

1 Set 6 (4-ounce) ramekins on a baking sheet and set aside.

2 In a small saucepan over medium-high heat, add the piloncillo and 2 tablespoons of water. Heat the piloncillo until fully melted, about 4 minutes, using a whisk to help the mixture break down. Continue cooking for another 2 minutes, or until the mixture darkens and begins to bub-ble. Quickly divide the caramel among the ramekins, swirling them gently to create an even layer of caramel. Set aside to cool and harden.

3 In a high-speed blender, add the cashew milk, coconut milk, coconut sugar, vanilla, chickpea flour, tapioca flour, agar agar, and salt and blend until completely smooth, about 1 minute. Transfer the mixture to a medium saucepan and set over medium heat. Cook, whisking frequently, until the mixture thickens slightly, about 5 minutes.

4 Divide the mixture among the ramekins. Cover and chill for at least 6 hours or overnight.

5 To release the flan from the ramekin, run a small knife around the outside of the custard. Invert a small plate onto the ramekin and flip the plate—the flan should release easily with the caramel sauce.

MAKES 1 (9-INCH) CAKE | 3 HOURS (PLUS 11 HOURS FOR CHILLING AND SOAKING) | GF, DF, V [OPTION]

Tres leches translates to "three milks," because the recipe is made with . . . three milks! Imagine our delight when we created a completely dairy-free recipe made with nut and coconut milks that gives you the same soft, caramel-y, melt-in-your-mouth layers as the original version. While we love using strawberries with the coconut whipped cream topping, fresh or canned sliced peaches are also traditionally used and can be substituted.

FOR THE CAKE

2 tablespoons melted coconut oil

3½ cups almond flour, plus more for dusting

1½ cups unsweetened almond milk

2 teaspoons fresh lemon juice

½ cup maple syrup

¼ cup unsweetened applesauce

1½ teaspoons vanilla extract

1 cup potato starch

⅓ cup tapioca flour

1½ teaspoons baking powder

1½ teaspoons baking soda

½ teaspoon sea salt

FOR THE TRES LECHES FILLING

1 (13.5-ounce) can full-fat unsweetened coconut milk

½ cup unsweetened almond milk

½ cup cashew milk

½ cup maple syrup

½ teaspoon vanilla extract

FOR THE COCONUT WHIPPED CREAM

2 (13.5-ounce) cans unsweetened coconut cream, chilled in the freezer for 40 minutes

2½ tablespoons powdered sugar

1 teaspoon vanilla extract

FOR THE STRAWBERRY TOPPING

2 cups fresh strawberries, hulled and sliced

2 tablespoons coconut sugar

1 Make the cake: Preheat the oven to 350°F. Grease 2 (9-inch) cake pans with the melted oil and dust the bottom and sides with almond flour. Shake out any excess flour and set aside.

continued

2 In a medium bowl, stir together the almond milk and lemon juice. Let it sit for 10 minutes to make a simple vegan buttermilk. You will notice that the milk slightly thickens and curdles just a bit. Stir in the maple syrup, applesauce, and vanilla.

3 In a large bowl, whisk together the almond flour, potato starch, tapioca flour, baking powder, baking soda, and salt. Add the wet ingredient mixture and gently whisk until smooth. The batter should be thick but pourable, like pancake batter.

4 Divide the batter among the prepared pans and bake on a center rack for 25 minutes, or until a toothpick inserted into the center comes out clean and the edges and surface are golden brown.

5 Let the cakes cool slightly in their pans, about 5 minutes. Invert the cake layers onto a wire rack to cool completely, preferably overnight or at least 6 hours, before assembling the cake. Cooling the cake will help it absorb the maximum amount of tres leches mixture.

6 **Make the tres leches:** In a medium saucepan over medium heat, add the coconut milk, almond milk, cashew milk, and maple syrup. Bring to a simmer, reduce the heat to low, and simmer gently for about 45 minutes, stirring frequently, until the mixture has thickened slightly and darkened in color. Remove the pan from the heat and whisk in the vanilla. If there are any lumps or if a thin film forms, whisk the mixture again or pass it through a sieve. Let the tres leches cool completely before assembling the cake.

7 **Make the coconut whipped cream:** In the bowl of a stand mixer fitted with the whisk attachment, add the chilled coconut cream, powdered sugar, and vanilla. Whip on high speed for 4 minutes, or until the mixture becomes thick and creamy.

8 **Make the strawberry topping:** In a small bowl, gently toss the strawberries with the coconut sugar. Let stand at room temperature for 10 minutes.

9 **Assemble the cake:** Set one of the cake layers on a serving plate. Using a toothpick or skewer, poke holes every ½ inch or so all over the cooled cake, taking extra care to pierce close to the edges and the middle of the cake. Gradually pour about half of the tres leches mixture all over the cake. Add the second cake layer and repeat, poking holes all over the cake and covering with the remaining tres leches mixture. Cover and refrigerate for 5 hours to let the cake soak.

10 Using an offset or silicone spatula, spread about half of the coconut whipped cream in an even layer on top of the cake. Chill the frosted cake for 10 minutes to let the whipped cream set. Frost the sides of the cake with the remaining whipped cream. Top the cake with the macerated strawberries and serve.

7

DRINKS/BEBIDAS

Since every morning at our house—come rain, shine, summer, or wintertime—starts **with a steaming cup of café con leche, we might say that all of our cherished family recipes were made possible and powered by the custom of this single drink.** It's a tradition that dates all the way back to when our mom was a young girl. Every morning, her dad, the "coffee server" of the household, would pour his wife and each of his kids a freshly brewed cup. While the kids got a cup of mostly milk and sugar with the tiniest dash of coffee, it was being included that made the ritual special. Coffee first, always.

If most of our gatherings involve food, then by extension, it's also accurate to say that the majority of our fondest moments have included great beverages too. That's why we wanted to dedicate a chapter of this book to the drinks you can reach for to accompany any occasion or meal—from washing down tacos with agua fresca, to curling up on the couch with a steaming hot mug of Mexican hot chocolate or atole de galleta, to celebrating with a few rounds of margaritas or Mexican martinis.

It's called "sharing a drink" for a reason—because drinks are best enjoyed with a tall pour of company. ¡Salud!

AGUA FRESCA DE JAMAICA
(ICED HIBISCUS TEA)

MAKES ABOUT 10 CUPS | 30 MINUTES | GF, DF, V

Every bit as refreshing as water, and every bit as flavorful as its vibrant hibiscus-red color suggests, this agua fresca is a popular choice among our family. It's available at nearly every restaurant and mom-and-pop shop in Laredo, and it was always on the top shelf of the fridge in tall pitchers in our childhood memories of playdates with friends.

7 cups boiling water

2 cups dried hibiscus flowers

2 cups sparkling water

⅔ cup maple syrup, plus more to taste

1½ cups fresh orange juice

⅓ cup fresh lime juice

Fresh mint sprigs, for garnish

1 In a large heat-safe bowl or saucepan, combine the boiling water and hibiscus flowers. Cover and let the flowers steep for 20 minutes.

2 Set a fine-mesh strainer over a pitcher and strain the mixture. Discard the flowers. Whisk in the sparkling water, maple syrup, orange juice, and lime juice. Taste and add more water or maple syrup if needed. Chill before serving. Serve over ice and garnish with mint sprigs.

TAMARIND, PINEAPPLE, AND GINGER AGUA FRESCA

MAKES ABOUT 8 CUPS | 45 MINUTES | GF, DF, V

There's something about this agua fresca that calls to mind a big foam cup, filled to the brim with ice, our favorite tacos or chips and guacamole, and a 90-plus-degree forecast. It's probably because the naturally sweet-and-sour flavor of the tamarind is so refreshing, making it one of the most popular agua fresca flavors. We tweaked the traditional list of ingredients slightly by adding fresh pineapple and zingy ginger—the ideal solution for when Mother Nature really brings the heat.

8 tamarind pods, hard shells and tough fibers removed

1 cup cubed fresh pineapple

1 (1-inch) piece of fresh ginger root, peeled

Pinch of sea salt

⅓ cup maple syrup, plus more if needed

3 cups of water

1 In a medium saucepan over high heat, bring 4 cups of water to a boil. Add the peeled tamarind pods, cover, and reduce the heat to medium. Cook for 30 minutes, stirring occasionally to press the pulp out of the pods. Uncover, remove the pan from the heat, and let the mixture sit for about 10 minutes to cool slightly.

2 Set a fine-mesh strainer over the pitcher of a blender. Strain the tamarind mixture into the blender, pressing gently with a spatula to release any remaining pulp from the pods. Add the pineapple, ginger, and salt and blend until completely smooth.

3 Strain the tamarind-pineapple mixture back into a pitcher. Add 3 cups of water and the maple syrup and stir until the maple syrup is fully dissolved. Taste and add more water or maple syrup if needed. Chill and serve over ice.

CASHEW HORCHATA

MAKES 10 CUPS | 15 MINUTES | GF, DF, V

You know a taqueria is going to be good when it's got the cooler of horchata sitting on the counter. This creamy, sweet, cinnamon-flecked drink is usually made with soaked rice and sweetened condensed milk, but our grain- and dairy-free version uses blended cashews to create a thicker consistency and maple syrup for sweetness.

10 cups of water, divided

1 cup raw unsalted cashews

2 whole cinnamon sticks (Mexican cinnamon, if you can find it)

½ cup maple syrup, plus more if needed

1 teaspoon vanilla extract

Pinch of sea salt

Ground cinnamon, for serving

1 In a high-speed blender, combine the cashews and cinnamon sticks with 2 cups of water and blend until completely smooth, about 5 minutes.

2 Transfer the cashew mixture to a cheesecloth set over a fine-mesh strainer or a nut milk bag. Working over a large bowl, twist the cheesecloth or nut milk bag closed and strain the milk through, kneading to help the liquid move around the solids. Discard the solids.

3 Transfer the liquid to a large pitcher and add 8 cups of water. Whisk in the maple syrup, vanilla, and salt, taste, and adjust for sweetness if needed. Chill before serving. Serve topped with a sprinkling of ground cinnamon.

AGUA DE LIMÓN WITH CHIA

MAKES ABOUT 10 CUPS | 30 MINUTES | GF, DF, V

In order to make it into the Agua Fresca Hall of Fame—or at least be one of our top picks—agua fresca has to be refreshing, cold, and packed with real fruit flavor. This limeade-like version definitely makes the cut with its bright citrus flavor and subtle sweetness. Plus the addition of chia seeds, which are naturally hydrating and get plump as they soak up the agua fresca. This juice also makes a great base for a paleta (page 153)!

8 cups cold water

½ cup fresh lime juice

½ cup maple syrup

2 tablespoons chia seeds

In a large pitcher, add the water, lime juice, and maple syrup and stir until the maple syrup has dissolved. Add the chia seeds and stir just briefly to combine. Chill the mixture for at least 30 minutes to let the chia seeds hydrate and plump up. Serve chilled, over ice.

PASSION FRUIT MARGARITA

MAKES 1 COCKTAIL | 5 MINUTES | GF, DF, V

When it comes to passion fruit, there's a lot to love about the way this tiny tropical fruit lends a bright, tart punch to recipes, from *nieves* (Mexican sorbets), to fruit cups, salsas, and—popularly—Mexican margaritas. Its tangy acidity pairs well with the sweetness of the agave and the earthy warmth of the tequila. We recommend serving this margarita on the rocks, in a glass rimmed with chile-lime seasoning.

1½ ounces passion fruit puree

1½ ounces tequila blanco

1 ounce fresh lime juice

1 teaspoon agave nectar

Chile-Lime Seasoning (page 210), or store-bought

In a cocktail shaker, add the passion fruit puree, tequila, lime juice, and agave and shake to combine thoroughly. Pour into a rocks glass filled with ice and rimmed with chile-lime seasoning.

MEXICAN MARTINI

MAKES 2 COCKTAILS | 10 MINUTES | GF, DF, V

If you're looking for something that's easy to make and easy to please, look no further than the Mexican martini—a crowd favorite here in Austin that combines tequila with olive brine, orange juice, and sometimes orange liqueur or lime juice. We've kept our version pretty close to the original, but you can customize as you see fit. It's hard to get this drink wrong!

½ ounce fresh lime juice, plus more for the rim

Sea salt, for the rim

2 ounces tequila blanco

2 ounces fresh orange juice

1 ounce Cointreau

1 ounce olive brine

Pitted green olives, for garnish

Rim 2 martini glasses with lime juice and salt. In a cocktail shaker, add the tequila, orange juice, Cointreau, olive brine, lime juice, and ice. Shake well and serve chilled or over ice. Garnish with the green olives.

PALOMA

MAKES 1 COCKTAIL | 5 MINUTES | GF, DF, V

Nine times out of ten, if our Siete family is getting together, palomas are on the menu. We love this cocktail for its light, bright flavor as well as its simple ingredients: grapefruit, lime juice, sparkling water, agave nectar, and tequila. Serve over ice with salt on the rim, or Chile-Lime Seasoning (page 210) if you want a (highly recommended) burst of spice.

2½ ounces fresh grapefruit juice

1½ ounces tequila blanco

1 ounce fresh lime juice

2 teaspoons agave nectar

3 ounces sparkling water

In a cocktail shaker, combine the grapefruit juice, tequila, lime juice, and agave and shake until thoroughly combined. Pour in a rocks glass over ice and top with the sparkling water.

CAFÉ DE OLLA CON LECHE

SERVES 4 | 20 MINUTES | GF, DF, V

This recipe is a blend between *café con leche* (coffee with sweetened milk) and *café de olla*, which is brewed coffee that is spiced with cinnamon and sweetened with *piloncillo*, or Mexican cane sugar. Finished off with a splash of dairy-free milk, this cozy, satisfying drink is perfect for energizing your mornings.

4 cups of water

2 ounces piloncillo

1 cinnamon stick (Mexican cinnamon, if you can find it)

1 whole clove

1 star anise (optional)

5 tablespoons ground dark-roast coffee

Dairy-free milk, for serving (oat milk tastes great with this)

1 In a medium saucepan over medium-high heat, combine 4 cups of water, the piloncillo, cinnamon, clove, and star anise, if desired, and bring to a boil. Reduce the heat to medium and cook, stirring occasionally, until the piloncillo dissolves completely, 3 to 5 minutes.

2 Remove the pan from the heat and stir in the coffee. Cover and let the coffee steep for 6 to 8 minutes, depending on how strong you'd like it. Using a fine-mesh strainer or a few layers of cheesecloth, strain the coffee mixture into a carafe and serve. You can also strain the coffee right into individual mugs. Serve with dairy-free milk to taste.

MEXICAN HOT CHOCOLATE

SERVES 2 | 15 MINUTES | GF, DF, V

When our extended family of aunts, uncles, and cousins gathers for Christmas, we always spend the evening huddled around the TV watching holiday movies. There are sweet treats like candies and Mexican wedding cookies for snacking, but the best part is the hot cocoa perfumed with cinnamon and the chile-spiked Mexican chocolate—which is also perfect for dunking desserts like Buñuelos (page 254) and Churros (page 156).

2 cups dairy-free milk (unsweetened almond or oat milk works well for this)

¼ cup coconut sugar

2 tablespoons unsweetened cocoa powder

½ teaspoon ground cinnamon

½ teaspoon vanilla extract

Pinch of sea salt

1 ounce stone-ground bittersweet Mexican chocolate, or other bittersweet chocolate

1 In a medium saucepan over medium heat, whisk together the dairy-free milk, coconut sugar, cocoa powder, cinnamon, vanilla, and salt. Cook, stirring occasionally, until very warm but not boiling, 5 to 7 minutes. Add the bittersweet chocolate and whisk until melted.

2 Divide between mugs and serve.

ATOLE DE GALLETA

SERVES 4 | 25 MINUTES | GF, DF, V

This rich, vanilla- and cinnamon-scented wintertime drink is a Mexican holiday tradition. With a flavor reminiscent of milk and cookies, it's the natural accompaniment to cold-weather rituals like sitting by a fire or warming your hands after playing in the snow. Although atole typically uses corn or masa to give it creamy body, our grain- and dairy-free version calls for using shortbread cookies instead.

1 teaspoon almond extract

1 (4.5-ounce) bag Siete Mexican Shortbread Cookies, or shortbread cookies of your choice

3 tablespoons maple syrup

1 cup unsweetened dairy-free milk, such as oat or almond

¼ teaspoon sea salt

Ground cinnamon, for garnish

1 In a medium saucepan over medium heat, combine 3 cups of water and the almond extract. Bring the mixture to a simmer and reduce the heat to medium-low, or low enough to maintain a gentle simmer.

2 Meanwhile, add the shortbread cookies to a high-speed blender and blend until finely ground, 1 to 2 minutes. Add the maple syrup, milk, and salt and blend until completely smooth.

3 Using a fine-mesh strainer, strain the shortbread mixture into the simmering water. Cook, whisking frequently, until the mixture has thickened slightly and resumes simmering, about 4 minutes. Do not bring the mixture to a boil or it will thicken too much. If you need to thin it out, you can add ¼ cup of water or milk as needed. Taste and adjust the sweetness to your liking.

4 Pour the atole into mugs and garnish with a pinch of ground cinnamon.

8

CONDIMENTS/CONDIMENTOS

Our family believes that you can judge the quality of a restaurant's food by the salsas on its tables. The idea is that the same level of care and attention that goes into preparing a dish should also go into the preparation of the condiments it's served with. Whether it's salsas, dips, toppings, spices, or pickles, the accompaniments to a meal can make all the difference between a regular dining experience and one that's exceptional.

This is especially true of Mexican cooking, where building layers of flavor and texture is the name of the game; condiments offer yet another crucial opportunity to infuse a dish with more dimension. Bright acidity from marinated onions and escabeche, earthy heat from chile oil, the cooling effect of rich and tangy cashew crema—these all work together to make a dish more than the sum of its parts. And then there are the salsas, which range from smoky salsa tatemada to fresh, herbaceous salsa cruda. Each has its own personality and complements a dish in its own unique way—lessons best learned through many repetitions of dipping, drizzling, and dousing.

In this chapter, we've included the recipes for our favorite condiments that regularly appear on our tables and are always stockpiled in our fridge. We highly recommend keeping some on hand, so that you can easily customize any dish to your preference.

CHILE OIL

MAKES 3 CUPS | 35 MINUTES | GF, DF, V

You can find this all-purpose condiment on our tables at most meals. It's a spicy and earthy blend of chiles, seeds, and oil, and makes pretty much anything (such as tostadas, tacos, rice and beans) tastier with just a drizzle.

NOTE: Although they're small, arbol chiles pack quite a punch! Stick with 2 if you like some heat, 3 if you want to turn things up.

4 dried guajillo chiles, stemmed and seeded

3 dried ancho chiles (about ½ ounce), stemmed and seeded

3 cups extra-virgin olive oil

½ cup blanched almonds

½ cup pumpkin seeds

2 tablespoons sesame seeds

2 dried arbol chiles

½ teaspoon dried Mexican oregano leaves or dried oregano leaves

2 teaspoons apple cider vinegar

1 teaspoon sea salt, plus more to taste

1 Add the guajillos and anchos to a dry cast-iron skillet or a comal (griddle) over medium heat. Toast, stirring and turning often to prevent burning, until the chiles start to darken in spots and start to puff up, 5 to 7 minutes. Transfer to a cutting board and roughly chop the chiles.

2 In a large saucepan over medium-low heat, heat the oil. Add the almonds, pumpkin seeds, and sesame seeds. Cook until the sesame seeds are golden and aromatic, 3 to 5 minutes. Add the chopped chiles and cook until they start to soften and change color, about 2 minutes. Stir in the arbol chiles and oregano and remove the pan from the heat. Let cool for about 10 minutes.

3 Transfer the mixture to a food processor and add the vinegar and salt. Pulse until the mixture is finely ground, 1 to 2 minutes. Taste and adjust the salt as needed.

4 Store the chile oil in a glass jar with a tight-fitting lid at room temperature for up to 1 month.

SALSA TATEMADA

MAKES ABOUT 2.5 CUPS | 35 MINUTES | GF, DF, V

While most of the grill at carne asadas is reserved for cooking meat, our family likes to take the opportunity to throw on some chiles, tomatoes, and onions, too, which are then blended to make this salsa. Of course, you can also char the vegetables on a comal or in a cast-iron skillet on the stovetop, but the char from the grill gives it a distinctly toasted and smoky flavor that pairs well with all the other grilled dishes and, of course, handfuls of salted tortilla chips!

1 teaspoon avocado oil

6 medium Roma tomatoes

¼ medium yellow onion, peeled

5 scallions, trimmed

5 garlic cloves, peeled

2 serrano chiles

¼ cup chopped fresh cilantro leaves

2 tablespoons fresh lime juice

¾ teaspoon sea salt

1 Heat a large cast-iron skillet or comal for 2 minutes over high heat. Add the oil and reduce the heat to medium. Add the tomatoes, onion, scallions, garlic cloves, and serranos to the pan and sear, turning occasionally, until well-charred, 10 to 15 minutes.

2 Transfer the tomatoes, onion, scallions, garlic, and serranos, plus the cilantro, lime juice, and salt, to a food processor and pulse until slightly chunky. Store in a sealed jar in the refrigerator for up to 2 weeks.

SALSA DE AIDA

MAKES ABOUT 3 CUPS | 10 MINUTES | GF, DF, V

Inspired by the many jars of salsa that our Grandma Campos had in the fridge at all times and on the table for every meal, Aida's version—aptly named "Aida's salsa"—has become a family staple. It's made from a short list of simple ingredients, which makes it perfect for those who don't want to plan ahead, like Aida. Blended to a smooth tomato-ey red, not only is it beautiful to look at, but it's so good that we say you could drink it too!

6 medium Roma tomatoes, roughly chopped

¼ medium white onion, roughly chopped

⅓ cup fresh lemon juice

2 tablespoons canned pickled jalapeño, seeded

½ teaspoon sea salt

½ teaspoon garlic powder

½ teaspoon onion powder

In a high-speed blender, combine the tomatoes, onions, lemon juice, pickled jalapeño, salt, garlic powder, and onion powder and blend until completely smooth. Store in a sealed jar in the refrigerator for up to 2 weeks.

CREAMY AVOCADO DIP

MAKES 2 CUPS | 10 MINUTES | GF, DF, V

At family gatherings, this cool, creamy dip lives next to the many bowls of salsas, cheeses, and guacamoles that take up almost an entire table on their own. The dip table is an oasis of food where we mingle, wait for the meat and mains, and load up our chips with pico de gallo, Salsa de Aida (page 202), warmed queso, and this dairy-free avocado dip. It also tastes great with fresh veggies and as a taco topping.

1 cup plain dairy-free yogurt

1 ripe avocado, cubed

Zest and juice of 1 lime

1 small garlic clove

½ teaspoon sea salt

¼ packed cup fresh cilantro leaves

In a high-speed blender, add the yogurt, avocado, lime zest and juice, garlic, and salt and blend until combined. Add the cilantro and blend until the dip is completely smooth. Store refrigerated in an airtight container for up to 1 week.

SALSA CRUDA

MAKES ABOUT 4 CUPS | 20 MINUTES | GF, DF, V

Salsa cruda is like a pico de gallo but smoother. It works equally well as a dip and as a condiment (especially for breakfast mariachis)! Be sure to use fresh lime juice in this recipe—it's very important to the quality of the salsa, and we always opt for using more rather than less.

8 medium Roma tomatoes, roughly chopped

½ medium red onion, roughly chopped

½ cup chopped fresh cilantro

¼ cup fresh lime juice

2 serrano chiles, stemmed, seeded, and roughly chopped

1 jalapeño chile, stemmed, seeded, and roughly chopped

1 teaspoon sea salt

In a food processor, combine the tomatoes, onion, cilantro, lime juice, serranos, jalapeño, and salt and pulse until the mixture reaches a chunky consistency. Store in a sealed jar in the refrigerator for up to 3 days.

CHILES TOREADOS

MAKES 1/2 CUP | 40 MINUTES | GF, DF, V

Go to any seafood or sushi restaurant in Laredo, and you will surely find chiles toreados. It's a unique condiment that blends blistered chiles with soy sauce and lime juice to make a spicy, acidic burst of umami that complements sushi or any raw fish dish.

3 serrano chiles

½ cup coconut aminos, tamari, or soy sauce

Juice of ½ lime

½ teaspoon sea salt

1 Add the serranos to a medium skillet over medium-high heat. Cook undisturbed for about 5 minutes, until charred on one side. Use tongs to turn the chiles and continue cooking and rotating until they're charred on all sides, about 15 minutes.

2 Transfer the charred chiles to a cutting board and slice them into thin rounds. Add the sliced chiles, plus the coconut aminos, lime juice, and salt, to a small jar. Let the mixture sit for at least 20 minutes before serving to let the flavors combine. Store in a sealed jar in the refrigerator for up to 1 week.

CASHEW CREMA

MAKES 2 CUPS | 30 MINUTES | GF, DF, V

Crema is a must-have condiment for Mexican dishes. It's the ying to salsa's yang, adding a layer of fat, sweetness, and acidity. So we came up with one that fit our family's nutritional needs by swapping out dairy for rich, creamy cashews. A drizzle of this crema makes any dish better—flautas, enchiladas, nachos, chilaquiles, and so on—and adds a little visual appeal when plating.

2 cups raw unsalted cashews

2 tablespoons fresh lemon juice

1 teaspoon sea salt, plus more to taste

1 In a medium saucepan over high heat, bring 6 cups of water to a boil. Reduce the heat to medium, add the cashews, and cook at a rapid simmer for 20 minutes.

2 Drain and rinse the cashews under running water and transfer them to a high-speed blender.

Add the lemon juice, salt, and 1½ cups of water. Blend until the crema is completely creamy, 1 to 2 minutes. Taste and adjust the seasonings as desired. The crema can be stored in an airtight container in the refrigerator for up to 2 weeks or in the freezer for up to 1 month. If freezing, make sure to blend the crema once it's thawed to emulsify it again

VARIATION
JALAPEÑO CREMA

Add ¼ cup of chopped fresh jalapeños along with the cashews, lemon juice, water, and salt. Puree until smooth, about 2 minutes.

CHAMOY

MAKES ABOUT 4 CUPS | 40 MINUTES | GF, DF, V

Chamoy, to put it simply, is a salsa for snacks, or *botanas*—a big part of Mexican-American food culture (which is why we devoted an entire chapter to them!). In Laredo, there are snack bars on every corner that feature chamoy on top of all sorts of different ingredients—fresh fruit, pickles, ice cream, a big pile of assorted gummy candies. Our chamoy is a unique blend of dried apricots, mangos, chiles, and lime and is sweet, salty, acidic, and spicy all at the same time. Pro tip: It's magical on the rim of a cocktail.

NOTE: Chamoy will continue to thicken due to the naturally occurring pectin in the fruit. Stir before serving and add a tablespoon of water to thin it out as needed.

---

2 tamarind pods, shelled

3 cups water

1 dried pasilla chile, stemmed and seeded

1 dried guajillo chile, stemmed and seeded

½ cup dried apricots

¼ cup prunes

¼ cup dried hibiscus flowers

½ cup maple syrup

½ cup plus 2 tablespoons fresh lime juice

1¼ teaspoons sea salt

1 In a small saucepan over high heat, add 1 cup of room-temperature water and the tamarind pods. Bring to a simmer, lower the heat, and cook for 5 minutes, stirring constantly to dissolve the tamarind pulp into the water. Strain the mixture over a medium bowl, catching any large tamarind seeds and passing as much pulp as possible. Add 2 cups of boiling water, pasilla, guajillo, dried apricots, prunes, and hibiscus flowers. Let the mixture sit, submerging the chiles, fruit, and hibiscus flowers as much as possible to soften them.

2 Transfer the mixture to a high-speed blender and add the maple syrup, lime juice, and salt. Blend on high speed until completely smooth and uniform, 1 to 2 minutes. Transfer the chamoy to an airtight container and let cool completely. Store in the fridge for up to 1 week.

CHILE-LIME SEASONING

MAKES 1/4 CUP | 15 MINUTES (PLUS 1 HOUR FOR BAKING) | GF, DF, V

If chamoy is a salsa for snacks, then chile-lime salt is the seasoning. It boasts the distinct flavor of Mexican chiles without the spice, is addictively acidic, and has a coarse saltiness that intensifies the flavor of anything you sprinkle it on. This seasoning miraculously makes watermelon taste even better—simply dust it over a juicy slice and you'll never look back. It is also the perfect match for the rim of your margarita glass. If you're like the kids in our family, you'll find that it's pretty great eaten straight out of your hand too!

3 tablespoons fresh lime juice

2½ tablespoons paprika

1 tablespoon cream of tartar

2 teaspoons cayenne pepper

1 tablespoon sea salt

1½ teaspoons coconut sugar

1 Preheat the oven to 170°F. Line a baking sheet with parchment paper and set aside.

2 In a small bowl, combine the lime juice, paprika, cream of tartar, and cayenne. Mix until an even paste forms. Spread the paste over the parchment so that it forms a rough 9 x 8-inch rectangle. Bake for 1 hour.

3 Allow the mixture to cool, then carefully scrape the paste into a mortar and pestle, molcajete, or small food processor. Add the salt and coconut sugar and mix until the mixture is fine and well combined. Store in an airtight jar in a cool, dry place for up to 1 week.

CHIPOTLE MAYO

MAKES 2 CUPS | 25 MINUTES | GF, DF, V

If you've ever had a fish taco, then it's likely you've had chipotle mayo. It's got a mild sweetness and tang with a generous amount of satisfying fat, but it's also got the complexity of smoky, spicy chipotles. Like chiles toreados, it goes well with seafood, but our chipotle-loving family believes it's good on most things like sushi, sandwiches, and drizzled on flautas.

2 cups raw unsalted cashews

2 tablespoons fresh lemon juice

2 canned chipotle chiles in adobo sauce

1 teaspoon sea salt, plus more to taste

1 In a medium saucepan over high heat, bring 6 cups of water to a boil. Reduce the heat to medium, add the cashews, and cook at a rapid simmer for 20 minutes.

2 Drain and rinse the cashews under running water and transfer them to a high-speed blender. Add the lemon juice, chiles, salt, and 1½ cups of water. Blend until the crema is completely creamy, 1 to 2 minutes. Taste and adjust the seasonings as desired. Store in a sealed jar in the refrigerator for up to 2 weeks, or freeze for up to 1 month. If freezing, make sure to blend the mayo once it's thawed to emulsify it again.

MARINATED RED ONIONS

MAKES ABOUT 2 CUPS | 15 MINUTES (PLUS 1 HOUR FOR MARINATING) | GF, DF, V

Marinated onions are a staple topping for any Mexican meal, and every family has their own recipe. When done just right, they add a sweet-acidic bite and a bit of crunch to any dish. Plus, with their neon fuchsia color, they also contribute a nice pop of color. We particularly like to add them to our tostadas, salads, and tacos.

1 small red onion, very thinly sliced (a mandoline works great here)

¼ cup fresh lime juice

¼ cup apple cider vinegar

1 teaspoon maple syrup

½ teaspoon sea salt

¼ teaspoon dried Mexican oregano leaves or dried oregano leaves

Pack the onions into a clean pint jar. Add the lime juice, vinegar, maple syrup, salt, oregano, and just enough water to cover, about ½ cup. Seal the jar tightly and shake to distribute the ingredients. Refrigerate for at least 1 hour before serving (overnight is ideal). These will keep for about 1 week in the refrigerator.

ESCABECHE

MAKES 1 QUART | 1 HOUR (PLUS 12 HOURS FOR CHILLING) | GF, DF, V

Is it a snack? Is it a condiment? Is it an accoutrement? The answer is D: All of the above. *Escabeche* means "pickled" in Spanish, and in this case, what's pickled is a mix of chiles, carrots, and onions. Escabeche can be added to dishes like tacos, tostadas, sandwiches, potato chips—or can be enjoyed straight from the jar. The brine is also a flavor powerhouse and can be used as a marinade, vinaigrette, or seasoning anytime you want to add a little brightness and kick to a dish.

---

2 tablespoons avocado oil

½ small red onion (about 4 ounces), sliced ½ -inch thick lengthwise

½ pound jalapeños (about 4 to 5 large jalapeños), sliced lengthwise in quarters, stems intact

½ pound medium carrots, peeled and cut into ¼-inch coins

1 cup distilled white vinegar

½ cup apple cider vinegar

2 dried bay leaves

2 tablespoons coconut sugar

2 sprigs of fresh thyme

2 sprigs of fresh oregano

4 whole allspice berries

½ teaspoon cumin seeds

1½ teaspoons sea salt

Freshly ground black pepper

1 Heat the oil in a large, shallow pan over medium-high heat. Add the onions and cook until slightly softened, 3 minutes. Add the jalapeños and carrots and cook, stirring occasionally, for another 5 minutes. Add the white vinegar, apple cider vinegar, bay leaves, coconut sugar, thyme, oregano, allspice, cumin, salt, and pepper to taste. Bring the mixture to a simmer and cook until the jalapeños turn a dull green and their skin starts to wrinkle in spots, about 10 minutes.

2 Remove the pan from the heat and let the mixture cool completely. Transfer the escabeche to a 1-quart glass jar, packing the jalapeños and onions tightly. Top with the cooking liquid and close with a tight-fitting lid. Refrigerate the escabeche for at least 12 hours before serving. Store in a sealed jar in the refrigerator for up to 2 weeks.

9

OPTIONS/OPCIONES

When we think about a great meal, it's really all about options. After we learned how it feels to miss out on some of our favorite foods because of dietary preferences and be left with fewer options—or none at all—we decided to start creating options of our own.

In this chapter you'll find some of our go-to alternatives for staples like masa and meats. Ensuring that everyone at the table has something deeply satisfying to enjoy has been a driving inspiration behind Siete, so it only made sense to bring that spirit to this book, too. There's grain-free masa, as well as a variety of savory plant-based "meat" fillings, whether you're going for spiced, ground, or shredded. These recipes are meant to give you a variety of satisfying choices—for both the recipes in this book and any other dish you might prepare at home. We promise you flavor, texture, and versatility—these recipes deliver on every front.

GRAIN-FREE MASA

10 MINUTES | GF, DF, V

Masa, or corn flour–based dough, is at the heart of many traditional Mexican recipes. This grain-free version is our substitution for traditional masa—a base we use to make everything from empanadas to tamales to buñuelos. You can combine the dry ingredients and store in a glass container to use whenever you need it—simply add water and you have your grain-free masa base.

2 cups almond flour

1¼ cups cassava flour

½ cup tapioca flour

1 teaspoon sea salt

1 cup of water

In a medium bowl, whisk together the almond flour, cassava flour, tapioca flour, and salt. Add 1 cup of water and use your hands or a wooden spoon to combine. Gently work the dough together with your hands to form a ball. If not using right away, wrap the masa in plastic wrap and store it in the refrigerator for up to 2 days. Before using, bring the dough to room temperature and knead again to soften it.

VEGAN "CHORIZO"

MAKES ABOUT 1 POUND | 45 MINUTES | GF, DF, V

In the Mexican-American kitchen, there are few aromas as assertively mouthwatering as the smell of chorizo frying in the pan. This chile-flecked, spice-packed, deeply flavored sausage is one of the meat staples in our cooking, showing up in many dishes—wrapped in tortillas, heaped on beans, topped with eggs, or doused with queso. It's not necessarily difficult to find a good store-bought vegan chorizo alternative, but most of these are made with soy. As an option for those who cannot or choose not to eat soy, we've developed our own version using pecans, chickpeas, and mushrooms.

TIP: Preparing the dried chiles before rehydrating them makes them easier to handle. Cut the chiles at the base of the stem with kitchen shears, remove the stem, and scrape or shake out most of the seeds and strings with your hands. You can also tear them with your hands—we recommend wearing disposable food-grade gloves if you go this route

6 dried guajillo chiles
(about 1 ounce), stemmed and seeded

2 dried ancho chiles
(about 1 ounce), stemmed and seeded

2 Medjool dates, pitted

¼ cup apple cider vinegar

4 garlic cloves, peeled and left whole

2 teaspoons dried Mexican oregano leaves or dried oregano leaves

1 teaspoon sea salt

1 teaspoon ground cumin

1 teaspoon cayenne pepper

2 whole allspice berries

½ teaspoon ground coriander

3 tablespoons avocado oil

1 recipe Vegan Ground "Meat" (page 222)

1 In a small saucepan, combine the guajillos, anchos, dates, and enough water to cover by about 1 inch. Bring to a boil over medium-high heat, pressing on the chiles to submerge them. Remove the pan from the heat, cover, and let stand until the chiles and dates are fully softened, 15 to 20 minutes. Reserve ¼ cup of the cooking liquid.

2 In a high-speed blender, combine the guajillos, anchos, dates, vinegar, garlic, oregano, salt, cumin, cayenne, allspice, coriander, and 2 tablespoons of the reserved chile-date cooking liquid. Puree until smooth, scraping down the blender occasionally. If needed, add another 2 tablespoons of the reserved cooking liquid to get a smooth but thick adobo. Set aside.

3 Heat the oil in a large nonstick or cast-iron skillet over medium heat. Add the ground "meat" mixture and cook until warmed through. Reduce the heat to low and pour the adobo sauce all over the mixture. Stir until completely coated. Cook until most of the liquid from the adobo has been absorbed by the chorizo mixture, about 10 minutes.

4 Cooked chorizo will keep covered in the fridge for 2 to 4 days, or you can freeze it for up to 1 month.

VEGAN GROUND "MEAT"

MAKES 1 POUND | 30 MINUTES | GF, DF, V

This recipe has nestled its way into the hearts of both the meat-eaters and vegans in our Siete familia. It started out as a simple vegetarian burrito filling option but quickly became what we reach for when it comes to tacos, flautas, and any other recipe that calls for ground meat. Texturally, it's a great alternative, and it packs a ton of savory flavor.

12 ounces white button mushrooms, trimmed

1 (15.5-ounce) can chickpeas, rinsed and drained

½ cup pecans

¼ cup plus 1½ tablespoons avocado oil

2 teaspoons nutritional yeast

1 teaspoon sea salt

½ teaspoon garlic powder

1 In a food processor, add the mushrooms and pulse until finely chopped. Transfer the mushrooms to a medium bowl and set aside.

2 Add the chickpeas and pecans to the food processor and pulse until finely chopped. Transfer the mixture to a medium bowl and set aside.

3 In a large cast-iron skillet over medium-high heat, heat 1½ tablespoons of the oil. Add the mushrooms and cook, stirring, for 1 minute. Add the chickpeas and pecans, reduce the heat to medium, and cook, stirring, for 5 minutes, or until most of the liquid from the mushrooms has evaporated. Add the nutritional yeast, salt, and garlic powder, plus ¼ cup of water, and cook for another 5 minutes, or until the liquid has evaporated. Add the remaining ¼ cup of oil, increase the heat to high, and cook, stirring frequently, for 4 to 5 minutes, until the mixture is crispy and resembles ground meat. Store in an airtight container in the refrigerator for up to 1 week.

VEGAN SHREDDED "MEAT"

MAKES ABOUT 28 OUNCES | 35 MINUTES | GF, DF, V

Revered for its firm, meat-like texture and its ability to soak up flavors from sauces, seasonings, and broths, jackfruit is a tasty plant substitute for animal proteins. Even though it's technically a fruit, its mild flavor and firm texture make it a great alternative option for pulled pork or chicken. This recipe is perfect to use as your go-to filling for flautas and enchiladas, and your go-to topping for tostadas and panchos.

2 (14-ounce) cans young jackfruit in water or brine, drained, rinsed, and thinly sliced

1½ teaspoons smoked paprika

¾ teaspoon sea salt

Freshly ground black pepper

¼ cup fresh orange juice

1 teaspoon coconut sugar

¼ cup avocado oil

2 garlic cloves, minced

1 In a medium bowl, add the jackfruit, paprika, salt, and pepper to taste. Set aside.

2 In a small bowl, whisk together the orange juice and coconut sugar. Set aside.

3 In a large cast-iron or stainless-steel skillet over medium heat, heat the oil. Add the jackfruit in an even layer and cook, undisturbed, for 10 minutes, only pressing down to release any moisture. Turn the jackfruit and add the garlic. Continue cooking, stirring occasionally, until golden brown, about 10 more minutes. Add the orange juice mixture and cook for 2 more minutes. Taste and adjust the seasonings as needed.

4 For a saucier consistency, add ¼ to ½ cup of water or vegetable broth along with the orange juice mixture. Cook until half of the liquid has been reduced, about 5 minutes. Taste and adjust the seasonings. Store in an airtight container in the refrigerator for up to 1 week.

10

MENUS FOR
GATHERING/REUNIONES

As people who value good company, we've never needed much of an excuse to get together with extended family, neighbors, and friends. There's an extra chair, an extra plate, an extra glass of agua fresca, and an extra helping of beans and rice at our table. But as we've gotten older, we've realized that even when the occasions for gathering come naturally, the art of hosting and cooking for a crowd is not always as simple as our mom and grandma made it look. From our epic weekend breakfast spreads, to our holiday traditions, to the casual yet expertly curated backyard barbecues, we sort of took for granted that all this food magically appeared from the kitchen. And not just that—it was always the perfect combination of dishes, each one complementing the next to make up one cohesive menu.

Now that we're inviting people into our own homes, we have a newfound appreciation for what goes into planning a meal that feels balanced and manageable. We also understand that with so many delicious-sounding yet potentially new-to-you recipes in this book, it may not feel intuitive when it comes to how to put them all together. That's why we've done some of the work for you. In this chapter, along with a few special recipes that we've saved for last, you'll find five menus for entertaining: Aida's Breakfast, Carne Asada, Border-Town, Holidays, and Siete-Style Large Gathering. While the specifics of your gathering may vary a bit from ours, we hope these menus offer some helpful tips and inspiration for pairings that make a complete meal.

AIDA'S BREAKFAST

When most people think about entertaining, their first thought is often "dinner." Or "fancy." Or hosting guests. But we'd argue that some of the most special family gatherings we've had took place around the breakfast table, especially when our mom would serve up all of our favorites—crispy papas smothered in salsa con queso (or "cheese sauce," as we call it), stacks of pancakes, refried beans, sweet conchas, and steaming-hot mugs of café de olla con leche. By the time we came barreling into the kitchen in our pajamas, there would be an impressive spread awaiting us. We'd linger at the table long after devouring everything we'd piled on our plates, too full and happy to move. Like reading the Sunday paper or watching Saturday-morning cartoons, this was a ritual we looked forward to at the end of every week.

Unlike gatherings that require extra planning and prep, the beauty of this menu is its simplicity. You can tailor the offerings by making fewer dishes, and most importantly, everyone serves themselves! PJs, slippers, and sleepyheads welcome.

AIDA'S SALSA CON QUESO*

SALSA DE AIDA
(PAGE 202)

CRISPY PAPAS
(PAGE 37)

REFRIED BEANS
(PAGE 131)

GRAIN-FREE PANCAKES
(PAGE 38)

CAFÉ DE OLLA CON LECHE
(PAGE 190)

AIDA'S SALSA CON QUESO

SERVES 4-6 | 20 MINUTES | GF

When we think of family traditions, right up there at the top of the list is Grandma Campos's cheese sauce. Our grandma would make this each time we would visit her house, and later, our mom made this with every one of her Saturday-morning breakfasts. We called it "cheese sauce," but it's similar to a cheesy salsa. Think: warm tomato salsa with onions and chiles and hunks of melty, gooey cheese mixed in. While it sounds very simple, there is definitely an art to making it! Over the years, many of us have tried re-creating it and have been disappointed with the outcome on our first try. The secret to getting it right is all about timing: Gently melt the cheese into the warm salsa, without stirring, so it gets soft, but doesn't dissolve.

Once ready, this nostalgic sauce can be poured into a bowl for dipping, used as a topping for tacos or scrambled eggs, or set out as a salsa for breakfast.

3 tablespoons avocado oil

5 Roma tomatoes, finely diced

½ cup white onion, finely diced

½ cup roughly chopped pickled jalapeños from Escabeche (page 215), or store-bought

¼ teaspoon onion powder

¼ teaspoon garlic powder

1 cup of water

Sea salt and freshly ground black pepper

8 ounces sharp cheddar cheese, or dairy-free cheddar cheese, cut into ½-inch cubes

1 Heat the oil in a medium skillet over medium heat. Add the tomatoes and onions and cook until the tomatoes start to soften, about 8 minutes. Add the pickled jalapeños, onion powder, and garlic powder with 1 cup of water and season with salt and pepper. Bring the mixture to a simmer and begin breaking apart the tomatoes by lightly mashing them with a wooden spoon. Reduce the heat to medium-low and place the cubed cheese in an even layer in the sauce. Simmer, covered, for about 30 seconds and remove from the heat. Let sit, covered, until the cheese is fully melted.

2 There should be melted pieces of cheese in the salsa, but not completely mixed in. Serve warm. Store any leftover queso in an airtight container in the refrigerator for up to 1 week and reheat in a skillet over medium heat. Serve with scrambled eggs, as a taco filling, or on its own.

CARNE ASADA

In Laredo, *carne asada* isn't just a taco filling; it's also what we call a cookout or a barbecue. As in: "See you at next Saturday's carne asada!" It's a common tradition in our Mexican-American culture, but our memories and the experience—watching columns of chipotle smoke rise up from the grill, smelling perfectly charred tortillas and savory charro beans, seeing little ones fall asleep on laps while others stay up and dance all night, and swapping stories and sharing laughs while fireflies twinkle nearby—are so much more.

When we were growing up, our dad would be at the grill, cooking a simple but tender beef fajita with lemon, spices, and steam. Our mom would be inside, preparing rice, beans, salsa, guacamole, and tortillas. Us kids would usually be running around with a tamarindo paleta in one hand, playing tag, and every so often running up to our dad in the hopes of a "sample-sized" piece of carne!

These days, our sister Becky's husband, Jorge, is the grill master—making meat and veggie *alambres*, or skewers, with rubs and marinades of every kind. Rob is typically at his side, beverage in hand, while Miguel playfully chases his daughter, nieces, and nephews around. Our mom still makes herself at home in the kitchen, but now Linda, Becky, and Veronica join her in making a feast from the sides alone. After all, more mouths to feed means "more is more!" The rest of us trickle in with our potluck contributions, spouses, children, old friends, and new stories to tell since the last family carne asada.

CARNE ASADA RUB*

CARNE ASADA MARINADE*

ALAMBRES (VEGETABLE SKEWERS)*

REFRIED BEANS
(PAGE 131)

ELOTES PREPARADOS
(PAGE 86)

MEXICAN RICE
(PAGE 134)

SALSA CRUDA
(PAGE 204)

PASSION FRUIT MARGARITA
(PAGE 184)

CARNE ASADA RUB

MAKES ABOUT 1/2 CUP, ENOUGH FOR 4 TO 5 POUNDS | 10 MINUTES | GF, DF, V

We remember the way our Grandma Campos would sift through her kitchen cabinet, intuitively mixing and matching the perfect seasoning for her chorizo. Our mom did just the same when making one of her carnitas-style dishes, using her taste, smell, and instinct to know exactly what each dish needed and how much. Veronica inherited that magic, having the ability to cook delicious food without measurements or a recipe. But for anyone who might be a little more by the book, we've included our favorite carne asada rub so that you can enjoy the same feeling of success.

NOTE: We prefer to use hanger steak, skirt steak, or boneless dark chicken meat with this rub, but you can also use your favorite vegetables.

2½ tablespoons sea salt

2 teaspoons cream of tartar

1½ teaspoons nutritional yeast

1 teaspoon coconut sugar

½ teaspoon freshly cracked black pepper

½ teaspoon dehydrated onion flakes

½ teaspoon garlic powder

½ teaspoon ground paprika

¼ teaspoon red pepper flakes

¼ teaspoon granulated dried orange peel

¼ teaspoon avocado oil

In a small bowl, combine the salt, cream of tartar, nutritional yeast, coconut sugar, black pepper, onion flakes, garlic powder, paprika, red pepper flakes, orange peel, and avocado oil. Season the steak generously with the spice mixture and grill to your liking. You can also store the rub in an airtight container at room temperature for up to 2 weeks.

CARNE ASADA MARINADE

MAKES 1 CUP, ENOUGH FOR 2 1/2 POUNDS | 10 MINUTES | GF, DF, V

When our sister Becky's husband, Jorge, is behind the grill, you know he's going to deliver an extravagant display of meats and veggies before the day is done. Our family's carne asada traditions have grown so much in size and splendor throughout the years, and everyone's favorite is Jorge's grilling. Still, we get nostalgic for the days when our dad would set up his grill in our childhood backyard, cook some beef fajita, and steam it in a pot with lemon and spices until it was perfectly tender. It was simple, but still so satisfying. Today, our secret to perfect carne asada is this marinade, which is a nod to our two favorite grill masters.

NOTE: We prefer to use hanger steak, skirt steak, or boneless dark chicken meat with this rub, but you can also use your favorite vegetables.

½ cup coconut aminos

½ cup chopped fresh cilantro

¼ cup fresh lime juice

2 tablespoons fresh orange juice

2 garlic cloves, chopped

1 teaspoon mild chile powder

½ teaspoon smoked paprika

½ teaspoon ground cumin

½ teaspoon sea salt

1 In a high-speed blender, add the coconut aminos, cilantro, lime juice, orange juice, garlic, chile powder, smoked paprika, cumin, and salt and pulse a few times to combine.

2 The marinade can be stored in the fridge in a sealed container for up to 1 week. When ready to use, submerge your meat or vegetables of choice in the marinade for 4 to 6 hours, or ideally overnight. Cook as desired.

ALAMBRES
(VEGETABLE SKEWERS)

MAKES 8 TO 10 SKEWERS | 45 MINUTES | GF, DF, V

To ensure we've got options for everyone at our carne asada, we like to make these veggie skewers. We slice up onions, bell peppers, zucchini, mushrooms—pretty much any vegetable we have in our fridge—thread them onto a skewer and grill them until they are decorated with the right amount of char, emitting a savory and smoky aroma from sitting atop the flames of the grill. Serve them over a plate of Mexican rice with a drizzle of salsa cruda, or slide everything into a tortilla for a veggie-packed taco.

---

1 poblano chile, stemmed, seeded, and cut into ½-inch pieces

1 green bell pepper, stemmed, seeded, and cut into ½-inch pieces

8 ounces white button mushrooms, cleaned and stems removed

1 pint cherry tomatoes

1 small red onion, peeled, quartered, and cut into 1-inch chunks

½ cup extra-virgin olive oil

½ cup finely chopped fresh cilantro

3 tablespoons fresh lime juice

2 teaspoons smoked paprika

1½ teaspoons sea salt, plus more to taste

1 teaspoon ground cumin

1 teaspoon coconut sugar

Freshly ground black pepper

1 If using wooden or bamboo skewers, soak the skewers in water for a minimum of 30 minutes or up to overnight to prevent them from burning. If using metal skewers, proceed with the recipe.

2 Group each vegetable separately on a baking sheet: the poblano, bell pepper, mushrooms, tomatoes, and red onion. Thread the vegetables onto the skewers, alternating each vegetable and doubling up on any extras, about 6 to 8 pieces on each skewer. Repeat with the remaining vegetables and skewers.

3 In a medium bowl, whisk together the oil, cilantro, lime juice, smoked paprika, salt, cumin, and coconut sugar. Pour all but ¼ cup of the dressing evenly over the vegetables. Reserve the remaining dressing. Marinate the skewers for 30 minutes to 1 hour at room temperature.

4 Prepare a grill or a cast-iron skillet over medium-high heat.

5 Working in batches, grill the skewers until the poblanos and bell peppers begin to soften and char, about 5 minutes for the first side. Continue cooking and turning frequently, about 10 minutes total.

6 Transfer the grilled skewers to a platter and drizzle with the remaining dressing. Season with salt and pepper.

MENU 3
BORDER-TOWN

Like the Mexican-American culture of Laredo, which exists on the southern border of Texas and northern Mexico, border-town food is also a mix of cuisines inspired by flavors, ingredients, and traditions of both cultures. We think of: mountainous plates of panchos assembled with fajita meat, refried beans, and cheese; shrimp cocktails in tall margarita glasses; cups of fresh fruit topped with chamoy and chile-lime seasoning; salty potato chips covered in hot sauce and lime juice; pirata tacos, overflowing with steak, beans, and queso; and agua fresca by the pitcher.

As a food-loving family, it's easy to identify the impact that growing up in Laredo has had on our palates and plates, and the foods we've since aspired to re-create and continue to eat. We're inspired by the flavors, customs, accessibility, and resourcefulness of border-town food, where a tortilla is what holds a taco together, but also a utensil for eating picadillo. Where leftover bacon grease goes into refried beans, eggs, and chorizo, and tortilla scraps are brought to life again into a delicious bowl of migas. We hope that this menu gives you a taste of our hometown, no matter where you live.

PANCHOS*

SHRIMP COCKTAIL
(PAGE 76)

FRUIT CUPS
(PAGE 89)

PAPITAS PREPARADAS
(PAGE 85)

PIRATA TACOS
(PAGE 59)

AGUA FRESCA DE JAMAICA
(PAGE 179)

PANCHOS

SERVES 4 | 45 MINUTES | GF, DF [OPTION]

Panchos are a lot like the familiar, comforting, and simple recipe for cheesy nachos that we know and love so well. They are similarly made with fresh tortilla chips and cheese, but have the distinctive addition of refried beans and fajita meat—beef, chicken, or both. (Between panchos and pirata tacos, you've got two tasty reasons to cook extra fajita at your next carne asada!) The beauty of this dish lies in your freedom to add dashes, dollops, or hearty servings of toppings to taste, which—in our experience—is the secret to clean plates all around!

½ teaspoon sea salt, plus more to taste

½ teaspoon ground cumin

½ teaspoon chile powder

½ pound skirt steak

6 Siete Grain Free Almond Flour Tortillas, or tortillas of your choice

1 tablespoon plus 2 teaspoons avocado oil

1 avocado, halved, pitted, and peeled

1 tablespoon finely chopped fresh cilantro

1 tablespoon fresh lime juice

1 cup Mexican blend shredded cheese or shredded dairy-free cheese of your choice

1 cup Refried Beans (page 131), or store-bought

1 Preheat the oven to 350°F.

2 In a small bowl, stir together the salt, cumin, and chile powder. Season the steak on both sides with the spice mixture. Set aside to rest at room temperature. (To make this ahead, you can season the steak and store in an airtight container, refrigerated overnight.)

3 Cut the tortillas into 8 wedges. Drizzle 1 tablespoon of the oil on a baking sheet and add the tortilla wedges in an even layer with no overlapping. Bake until golden and crispy, 8 to 10 minutes. Transfer the chips to a large bowl and toss with salt to taste. Reserve the baking sheet; you'll use it again shortly.

4 In a large cast-iron skillet over medium-high heat, heat the remaining 2 teaspoons of oil. Add the steak and cook for 4 to 5 minutes per side, until it reaches a medium doneness. Transfer the steak to a cutting board, cover with foil, and let rest for 10 minutes. Cut across the grain into wide strips, then cut the strips into 1-inch cubes.

5 Add the avocado to a medium bowl and mash it lightly with a fork. Add the cilantro, lime juice, and salt to taste and continue mashing and stirring until combined.

6 Arrange half of the chips on the baking sheet and drizzle half of the shredded cheese on top. Dot half of the refried beans around and on top of the chips and cheese, followed by half of the steak cubes. Drizzle any cutting board juices over the steak. Repeat with the remaining chips, shredded cheese, beans, and steak.

7 Bake the nachos until the beans and cheese are heated through and softened, 7 to 10 minutes. Serve topped with scoops of the guacamole.

MENU 4
HOLIDAYS

They say there's no place like home for the holidays, and we believe this to be true. In our family, we start celebrating our favorite holiday, Christmas, in July. Becky starts listening to Christmas music and watching classic Hallmark movies, while Miguel keeps the Christmas lights strung up at his house from the last year.

When December finally rolls around, all the kids and grandkids come to Aida and Bobby's house on the same day. Boxes filled with ornaments line the living room, and everyone unpacks their favorites, placing them on the tree and singing along to Christmas music. Becky and Linda's collection of two hundred–plus nutcrackers fills every inch of shelving. A toy train chugs around colorful presents and fuzzy socks.

Feasting on Christmas Day starts with one of Mom's special breakfasts, which takes place closer to lunchtime. Eggs, pancakes, potatoes, salsa, beans, biscuits—there are usually ten or more dishes to choose from. After presents have been opened and bellies have been stuffed, we spend the rest of the day enjoying time together, watching movies, and helping the kids set up their new gadgets. Later in the evening, we fill the table with an array of holiday foods. Mom's brisket, tamales, and empanadas—and the long-awaited, ceremonious dessert, buñuelos. We pass them around, each person breaking off a piece, uttering *mmms* as they melt in our mouths. We follow each bite with a sip of steaming Mexican hot chocolate, savoring the last moments of the meal we look forward to all year.

TAMALES*

SPAGHETTI VERDE*

SAVORY EMPANADAS*

BUÑUELOS*

RED PORK OR CHICKEN POZOLE
(PAGE 56)

ATOLE DE GALLETA
(PAGE 194)

MEXICAN HOT CHOCOLATE
(PAGE 193)

TAMALES

MAKES 12 | 6 HOURS | GF, DF

Holidays at Grandma Campos's house were always a flurry of activity, but amid the chaos you would find a highly organized assembly line for making tamales. Anyone who could see over the kitchen counter would become part of the line, spreading masa on corn husks while Grandma Campos made the fillings.

If you're preparing a batch of these with your own crew of helpers, it's a good idea to make the masa ahead of time; it can be kept in a bowl covered with a damp cloth at room temperature for up to 4 hours. You can also make it the night before and store it in the fridge—just give it a stir when you're ready to use it.

NOTE: If making both fillings, double the masa preparada recipe to make 24 tamales, (1 dozen for each filling). It's important not to skip the final step. Leave these at room temperature one hour after cooking! This helps the tamales cook completely.

FOR THE BEEF FILLING

1½ pounds beef chuck roast or skirt steak

½ medium yellow onion

1 dried bay leaf

1½ teaspoons sea salt, plus more to taste

1 ounce dried guajillo chiles
(about 6 chiles), stemmed and seeded

1 cup canned tomato puree

4 garlic cloves, peeled and left whole

2 tablespoons apple cider vinegar

1½ teaspoons dried oregano

½ teaspoon ground cumin

FOR THE BEAN AND JALAPEÑO FILLING

1½ cups Refried Beans (page 131),
or store-bought

12 pickled or fresh jalapeño slices

FOR THE MASA PREPARADA

1 recipe Grain-Free Masa (page 219)

1 cup non-hydrogenated all-vegetable
shortening or coconut shortening

1 tablespoon baking powder

FOR THE TAMALES

12 banana leaves or corn husks (about
10 x 6 inches), plus 5 more for lining
the steamer and tying tamales

Salsa Tatemada (page 201), for serving

continued

1 **Make the beef filling:** In a large stockpot over medium-high heat, combine the beef, onion, bay leaf, salt, and enough water to cover. Bring to a simmer, reducing the heat as needed to maintain the simmer and skimming off any foam that rises to the surface. Cook until the beef is tender when pierced with a fork, 50 to 60 minutes. Reserve 1 cup of the cooking broth and save the rest for another use.

2 Remove the pot from the heat and transfer the beef to a large bowl to cool. Set the pot aside; you'll use it again later. Trim off any excess fat from the beef, then finely shred it. Transfer the beef to a medium bowl and set aside.

3 In a small saucepan over medium-high heat, add the chiles and enough water to cover by about 1 inch. Bring to a boil, pressing on the chiles to keep them submerged. Remove the pan from the heat, cover, and let stand until the chiles are fully softened and pulpy, 15 to 20 minutes.

4 Using a slotted spoon, transfer the chiles to a high-speed blender. Discard the soaking water. Add the tomato puree, garlic, vinegar, oregano, cumin, and the reserved beef cooking broth. Puree until completely smooth.

5 Return the shredded beef to the reserved stockpot over medium heat. Pour the guajillo salsa all over the meat, mixing to coat the meat completely. Season with salt and cook, stirring often to encourage the meat to fall apart into shreds. Continue cooking until the sauce is thick and the meat has absorbed some of the sauce, about 20 minutes. Remove the pot from the heat and cover until you're ready to assemble the tamales.

6 **Make the bean and jalapeño filling:** In a small saucepan over low heat, add the refried beans and 2 tablespoons of water at a time to thin them out slightly, about the consistency of hummus. Cook until heated through, about 5 minutes. Remove the pan from the heat and cover to keep warm.

7 Place the pickled or fresh jalapeños into a small bowl.

8 Make Grain-Free Masa recipe (page 219).

9 In the bowl of a stand mixer fitted with the paddle attachment, add Grain-Free Masa and shortening. Beat on medium-high speed until fluffy and creamy, about 2 minutes.

10 Reduce the mixer speed to low and add the baking powder and the remaining 1½ teaspoons of salt. Gradually add the masa dough in pieces and beat on low speed until well combined and smooth, 3 to 5 minutes, stopping occasionally to scrape down the sides of the bowl. The masa preparada should have the consistency of thick frosting. Cover the bowl with a damp towel and set aside.

continued

11 **Assemble the tamales:** Working with one banana leaf at a time, warm the banana leaves over a medium-high flame on a gas burner, turning often with tongs, until the leaves are glossy and pliable, about 10 seconds. Alternatively, you can microwave the banana leaves on high power, 6 at a time on a microwavable plate, in 10-second intervals until the leaves are glossy and pliable, about 30 seconds.

12 If using corn husks, add the corn husks and enough water to cover to a large stockpot. Weigh down the husks by placing a molcajete or a small pot on top to completely submerge the husks. Bring the water to a boil over high heat, then remove the pot from the heat. Cover the pot and let the husks soak for at least 1 hour, or up to overnight.

13 Place a banana leaf on a clean work surface with one short end closest to you. Using the back of a spoon, spread about ¼ cup of the masa preparada lengthwise in the center of the leaf in a 5-by-4-inch rectangle of even thickness.

14 If using corn husks, remove the husks from the pot, shake off any excess water, and pat dry with a kitchen towel. Start with the wide end of the corn husk closest to you. Using the back of a spoon, spread about ¼ cup masa preparada lengthwise in the center of the corn husk and work out toward the edges, leaving a clean ½-inch border at the top without masa.

15 If using beef filling, spoon about 2 tablespoons of the filling in the center of the masa. If using bean and jalapeño filling, add 2 tablespoons of beans and 1 slice of jalapeño.

16 For the banana leaves, wrap the leaf around the filling until you have a small rectangle that's sealed on all sides. (You shouldn't be able to see any of the filling.)

17 For the corn husks, fold one side of the husk over so that the masa encases the filling. Fold the top end of the corn husk down toward the center and roll to wrap the remaining husk around the tamale, leaving the bottom end open. Repeat with the remaining husks, spreading the masa preparada, adding the filling, and rolling up the tamales.

18 Fill a large stockpot with 1 inch of water and drop a small spoon into the water. (The spoon will rattle while the water simmers steadily, and if you run out of water, the spoon will stop rattling and alert you to add more.) Place a steamer insert (at least 7 inches deep) in the stockpot, ensuring the water does not touch the bottom of the steamer. Line the bottom and sides of the steamer with the remaining corn husks or banana leaves. Stand the tamales vertically in the steamer, with open ends up, in a tightly packed single layer.

19 Set the pot over medium-high heat until steam is visible, 6 to 8 minutes. Cover the tamales with two clean, damp kitchen towels to trap the heat, then cover tightly with a lid. Reduce the heat to low and cook for 1 hour and 30 minutes. Check the water level halfway through and add more water as needed. Remove the pot from the heat and let the tamales rest for 1 hour before unfolding.

20 To test doneness, carefully uncover the pot and remove 1 tamale. It should be soft in the middle but not runny. If it's not cooked completely, return the tamales to the heat for an additional 30 minutes. Turn off the heat and let the tamales sit for another hour before unfolding them. Serve the tamales hot with salsa tatemada.

21 Wrap leftovers tightly in reusable plastic bags and keep in the refrigerator for up to 3 days. To reheat, steam them wrapped and covered with a damp cloth for 15 to 20 minutes.

SPAGHETTI VERDE
(GREEN SPAGHETTI)

SERVES 4 | 1 HOUR 30 MINUTES | GF, DF, V

This festively colored dish is synonymous with Thanksgiving and Christmastime feasting in Laredo. It is reminiscent of spaghetti alfredo because of its creamy sauce but gets its herbaceous, earthy flavor from ingredients like cilantro, charred poblanos, and pumpkin seeds. Unlike the more traditional spaghetti we enjoyed on weeknights when we were tight on prep time and ingredients, this recipe is a little more involved—but the payoff is getting to experience this beloved (and dairy-free) recipe that many South Texans share a fondness for.

FOR THE HERBY PEPITA PARMESAN

½ cup pumpkin seeds, toasted in a dry skillet until fragrant

½ cup fresh cilantro leaves

1 tablespoon nutritional yeast

½ teaspoon sea salt

FOR THE VERDE SAUCE

2 poblano chiles

½ cup raw unsalted cashews

2 tablespoons vegan butter

½ cup roughly chopped white onion

6 garlic cloves, sliced

2 teaspoons sea salt

1 cup unsweetened almond milk

1 tablespoon nutritional yeast

2 teaspoons fresh lemon juice

1 pound gluten-free spaghetti of your choice

Freshly ground black pepper

1 Make the Parmesan: In a high-speed blender or food processor, add the pumpkin seeds, cilantro, nutritional yeast, and salt and pulse just a few times, until finely ground, being careful to avoid turning the mixture into a paste. You may also use a molcajete to grind it. Transfer to a small bowl and set aside.

2 Make the sauce: Using tongs, char the poblanos directly on the stovetop over high heat until blackened in spots, about 5 minutes per side. Transfer the charred poblanos to a bowl and cover immediately with a plate to create steam and loosen up the tough skins. Let the poblanos sit and steam for 10 minutes. When cool enough to handle, rub your fingers over the poblanos to peel off as much as possible. Discard the skins, stems, and seeds. Slice the poblanos into large strips and set aside. (You can also char the poblanos under the broiler. Position a rack as close to the broiler as possible and char the poblanos for 8 to 10 minutes, until blackened on all sides, turning halfway through to achieve even charring. Steam and continue prepping the charred poblanos as above.)

3 In a small saucepan over high heat, bring 2 cups of water to a boil. Add the cashews and lower the heat to medium. Gently cook the cashews for 20 minutes. Drain the cashews and rinse well.

4 In a large skillet over medium heat, heat the vegan butter. Add the onion and cook until translucent, about 4 minutes. Add the sliced poblanos, garlic, and 1 teaspoon of the salt. Cook until the garlic is fragrant, about 3 more minutes. Remove the pan from the heat.

5 Transfer the poblano mixture to a blender along with the cooked cashews, almond milk, nutritional yeast, lemon juice, and remaining 1 teaspoon of salt. Blend for at least 2 minutes, until completely smooth and creamy but pourable, like heavy cream.

6 Cook the pasta according to the package directions. Drain the pasta and transfer to a large bowl. Pour the poblano sauce all over the pasta and toss vigorously to coat. Top the pasta generously with the herby pepita parmesan and black pepper. Serve immediately.

SAVORY EMPANADAS

MAKES 12 EMPANADAS | 1 HOUR 45 MINUTES | GF, DF, V [OPTION]

Every holiday season, our mom leads the charge of making a variety of empanadas, both sweet and savory. Then, as is tradition, all of us, along with every one of the grandchildren, join her to cut, shape, and fill the dough before closing up the empanadas and gently crimping the edges with a fork. We've perfected the production line and can churn out what seems like hundreds of empanadas with fillings ranging from chorizo, beans, and picadillo to apple, pecan, and peach. This is a classic recipe for beef and potatoes, though you can easily use our ground meat substitute, or any other fillings of your choice. Making these is an involved process, but they make for a fun and festive meal that gets the whole family in the kitchen.

NOTE: Because this is a grain-free dough, it will be delicate to work with and tearing is normal. If your dough does tear while shaping the empanadas, you can just patch it back together.

---

2 tablespoons avocado oil, or your favorite oil for frying, plus more

½ small white onion, finely diced

4 garlic cloves, minced

1 small Yukon Gold potato, finely chopped

1 carrot, peeled and finely diced

1/2 pound 80/20 ground beef or Vegan Ground "Meat" (page 222)

2 teaspoons sea salt (1 teaspoon for Vegan Ground "Meat"), plus more to taste

¼ cup chopped pecans

2 tablespoons pickled jalapeños, from Escabeche (page 215), or store-bought, finely diced

Freshly ground black pepper

1 recipe Grain-Free Masa (page 219)

Salsa Tatemada (page 201), or salsa of your choice, for serving

1 In a large skillet over medium-low heat, heat the oil. Add the onions and garlic and cook for 10 to 15 minutes, until the onions are soft. Add the potatoes and carrots and cook until the potatoes are tender, about 8 minutes. Add the ground beef and 2 teaspoons of the salt, or vegan ground meat and 1 teaspoon of the salt, increase the heat to medium, and break up the meat with a wooden spoon. Cook until the meat is cooked through, or warmed through if using vegan meat.

2 Add the pecans and pickled jalapeños, season with salt and pepper, and cook for 5 minutes. Remove the pan from the heat and set aside.

3 Divide the base masa into 12 pieces. Roll each piece into a ball and press in a tortilla press lined with parchment paper or plastic wrap. If you do not have a tortilla press, cut two sections of parchment or a plastic disposable bag into large enough squares to press dough, about 7 inches by 7 inches wide. Dust the plastic sheets with cassava flour and place a dough ball into one piece of floured plastic or parchment. Cover the dough with another layer of parchment or plastic and roll each dough into a round circle using a rolling pin. Repeat with each of the remaining dough balls. Fill each empanada with about 2 tablespoons of the filling in the center. Fold the dough over and lightly press the seams to close the empanada. Lay the assembled empanadas on a clean kitchen towel and cover with another kitchen towel to keep from drying out. Repeat with the remaining masa and fillings.

4 In a high-sided cast-iron skillet over medium-high heat, heat about 3 inches of oil to 350°F.

5 Working in batches, fry the empanadas for 2 to 3 minutes, or until golden brown. Carefully transfer the fried empanadas to a wire rack to cool before serving.

6 Serve with the salsa.

BUÑUELOS

MAKES 8 BUÑUELOS | 1 HOUR | GF, DF, V

For three generations, our family has honored the tradition of enjoying buñuelos every Christmas and New Year's Eve. As a child, our mom would watch her Grandma ChaCha roll out the dough, stretch it over her knee, plop it in the fryer, and sprinkle it with cinnamon and sugar. By all accounts, her secret recipe was melt-in-your-mouth delicious. This holiday ritual continued with our mom and Grandma Campos, and then again with us when we were children. In recent years, we developed a gluten-free variation so we can continue to observe this beloved tradition.

¼ cup coconut sugar

2 teaspoons ground cinnamon

1 recipe Grain-Free Masa (page 219)

Avocado oil, or your favorite oil for frying

Flaky salt, for finishing

1 In a small bowl, whisk together the coconut sugar and cinnamon. Set aside.

2 Lay out a kitchen towel on the counter. Divide the dough into 8 equal pieces and roll the pieces into small balls. Using a tortilla press, flatten the dough balls into roughly 6-inch disks. Carefully transfer each disk to the kitchen towel while you press the remaining dough.

3 In a high-sided cast-iron skillet over medium-high heat, heat 1 to 2 inches of avocado oil to 350°F. Set a wire rack over a baking sheet and place it nearby for draining.

4 Fry each disk of dough for about 2 minutes per side, until golden and crisp. Transfer the buñuelos to the rack and sprinkle generously with the cinnamon-sugar mixture. Top with flaky sea salt, if desired. Serve immediately.

SIETE-STYLE LARGE GATHERING

Over the years, our family has grown from seven to Siete, and beyond. Our gatherings these days look a lot like our meals did growing up, only at a much longer table. We are surrounded by people who have taken our family mission, made it their own, and helped Siete grow, and sitting down and eating together is a precious occasion made regular and casual.

At Siete, we've made a tradition of Friday Lunches. Our entire Austin team gathers for a family-style meal—there are no rules for the menu other than there has to be plenty to go around and options to satisfy everyone's dietary preferences. It's a special feeling to pause collectively at the end of the week in order to slow down and connect.

While lunch may not be the obvious choice of meals to host a get-together, it's the perfect time to serve up a relaxed, informal spread that includes some of our favorite crowd-pleasers.

We hope this menu, assembled with recipes that our Siete family can never get enough of—like grain-free fried chicken, shrimp tostadas, Mexican chopped salad, and palomas—inspires you to gather with us in salud, sabor, and spirit. There's something for everyone, and everyone's invited.

GRAIN-FREE FRIED CHICKEN OR MUSHROOMS·

SHRIMP TOSTADAS
(PAGE 68)

CHILE OIL
(PAGE 199)

POBLANO RICE
(PAGE 136)

MEXICAN CHOPPED SALAD
(PAGE 148)

PECAN PIE EMPANADAS
(PAGE 167)

PALOMA
(PAGE 188)

GRAIN-FREE FRIED CHICKEN OR MUSHROOMS

SERVES 4 | 1 HOUR 45 MINUTES | GF, DF, V [OPTION]

Our family loves fried chicken—we're from South Texas, after all! So it was only natural that we come up with a gluten-free alternative that still manages to be crispy on the outside and tender and juicy on the inside. Whether you're making this recipe with chicken or mushrooms, the effect is the same: a savory, spicy hit of Southern charm.

¾ cup Cashew Crema (page 207)

1 teaspoon sea salt

1 teaspoon smoked paprika

1 teaspoon granulated garlic

2½ pounds boneless, skinless chicken thighs

1 cup tapioca flour

Avocado oil, or your favorite oil for frying

Chile Oil (page 199), for serving

Chile-Lime Seasoning (page 210),
or store-bought, for serving

Flaky sea salt, for serving

1 In a large bowl, whisk together the cashew crema, salt, ½ teaspoon of the smoked paprika, ½ teaspoon of the granulated garlic, and 2 tablespoons of water until smooth. Add the chicken and toss to coat. Cover and refrigerate for at least 1 hour and up to 3 hours.

2 In a medium bowl, whisk together the tapioca flour, the remaining ½ teaspoon of smoked pa-

prika, and the remaining ½ teaspoon of granulated garlic.

3 Line two baking sheets with parchment paper and set a wire rack on top of one of the lined sheets. Set aside.

4 Working with one piece of chicken at a time, remove the chicken from the marinade, shake off any excess marinade, and toss in the tapioca flour mixture to coat thoroughly. Lay the coated chicken on the lined baking sheet and repeat with the remaining chicken.

5 In a high-sided, heavy-bottomed skillet or Dutch oven, heat about 1½ inches of avocado oil to 350°F.

6 Working in batches, carefully lay the coated chicken in the hot oil. As the chicken cooks, control the temperature of the oil so that it levels off at around 350°F so the chicken cooks thoroughly. Fry for 7 to 10 minutes, until the thickest part of the thigh reaches an internal temperature of 165°F.

7 Use tongs to transfer the fried chicken to the wire rack and repeat with the remaining chicken. Let the chicken rest for at 3 to 5 minutes before serving.

8 Transfer the chicken to a serving platter and finish with the chile oil, chile-lime seasoning, and a touch of flaky salt.

VARIATION
CHICKEN-FRIED MUSHROOMS

Cut 1½ pounds of chicken of the woods or oyster mushrooms in 2- to 3-inch pieces. Marinate as above. You can dredge as above and fry immediately or marinate for up to 1 hour, then dredge and fry. Cooking time is a little shorter, 5 to 7 minutes. Finish with the chile oil, chile-lime seasoning, and flaky salt.

ACKNOWLEDGMENTS

To our Siete community, whether this is our first time meeting or you were among the first to pick our almond flour tortillas off the shelves of Wheatsville some eight years ago (or we were introduced fatefully anytime in between). For every one of you who have come across our family's favorite foods and have been inspired to get into the kitchen to create a meal made for sharing, with enjoyment and inclusivity in mind: This is our dream, and you have made it a reality. Thank you for inviting us into your home, kitchen, table, and heart. And for all of you who excitedly suggested that we make a family cookbook—you know who you are—we received your requests with happy hearts, and take so much joy in sharing this book with you.

To the amazing team that celebrated our vision for this book and helped bring it to life. To Nicole Tourlet, our awesome agent, who patiently and expertly mentored us through so many new learning curves: We wouldn't have even known where to start without you. To Julie Will, our brilliant publisher: Thank you for believing in our recipes, stories, and hopes for this book. We're honored to be a part of the renowned Harper Wave family and to learn from your generous expertise. To our sage editor and co-writer, Rachel Holtzman: Thank you for going through this book with a fine-tooth comb, and ensuring excellence on every page. To our masterful photographer, Kristin Teig, who filled this cookbook with photos we will obsess over forever (forever!)—thank you for captur-

ing the essence of Siete and weaving precious Garza family heirlooms throughout the book. To Maria Del Mar Cuadra, our thoughtful stylist, who taught us tricks of the trade, thank you for making the photoshoot process so fun and easy-breezy, and continuing to delight our team with equipment and tips after it was all said and done. To David Peng, our creative and supportive styling assistant: Thank you for bringing your calm and patient presence to the set, and for helping get our photography team through the finish line. To Paola Briseño and Jeanelle Olson, our recipe developers: You both are stars. Thanks for adopting our food philosophy to help re-create family recipes with ingredients for all to enjoy—and on a dime! When we say that we could not have done it without you, we mean it. Thank you all for embracing our nuances and teaching us all the intricacies there are to creating a book that we could be as proud of as we are of this one. And to our Siete cookbook team: Thank you for working tirelessly from start to finish.

To the incredible people who not only want to hang out with us every day, but also work alongside us to make our favorite foods nourishing, delicious, and available: We could not have hoped for a better group of people to call "familia," since each and every one of you is a true extension of our family. We are humbled that our lives have intertwined, and that you've willingly signed up for "togetherness" as a way of life. Thanks for everything.

To our strong, supportive, and loving Laredo friends, family, community, and city: We are honored to call "the 956" our hometown, and we share so many wonderful childhood memories in your company. We hope the stories of Laredo feel like a playful nudge to you and the city we'll always call "home" and the place we always look forward to visiting for its great food and even greater company. Biased as we may be, our vibrant and dynamic border-town culture—present in every restaurant, store, shop, and Laredoan—is unlike any other, and we carry that pride with us wherever we roam.

To our mom, who embodies love for all, through your warm hugs, the way you share magical snacks and meals, and the way you in-spire kindness and inclusivity around the table and beyond. You are an example to us all. We will never be able to thank you enough.

To our ancestors, who paved the way for us, through sacrifice and bravery: We're forever grateful for your steadfast devotion to giving your family opportunity and possibility. For instilling in us the value of education—something that's been passed on from generation to generation. To our Grandpa Tony Campos—the epitome of strength, reliability, and selflessness: You are an inspiration, and we aspire to lift people up the way you did throughout your career. And our Grandma Alicia Campos, who is everywhere in this cookbook—from the stories and the recipes, to the photographs that include her hand-stitched tablecloths. Even though you cooked without writing down your recipes, your warmth and brilliance are woven into the details and legacy of this book. To our aunts, uncles, cousins, spouses, and friends that are family, who have lent us their time, skills, and support since day one: Your kind generosity, unwavering support, and unparalleled enthusiasm mean the world to us.

To our beautiful, vibrant, and welcoming Mexican-American heritage, which has made us who we are: Our heritage continues to influence the way we eat, invite, gather, honor, remember, and celebrate. It inspires and represents what we want to create and put out into the world. It's a north star to our company culture, family values, Siete products, and mission. It reminds us of where we came from, informs how we give back, and shapes how we grow. It allows us to express our true and authentic selves. We're grateful for the way that it continually builds our amazing community, fosters a sense of family near and far, and brings people together around the table.

INDEX

(Page references in *italics* refer to illustrations.)

A

adobo, 7
Adobo (recipe in Vegan Chorizo), 220–21
Agua de Limón with Chia, *179*, 183
agua fresca:
  de Jamaica (Iced Hibiscus Tea), 178, *179*
  Tamarind, Pineapple, and Ginger, *179*, 181
Alambres (Vegetable Skewers), 236–37
almond flour, 7, *13*
  Apple Empanadas, *164*, 165–66
  Grain-Free Pancakes, 38, *39*
  Masa, Grain-Free, *218*, 219
  Masa Preparada for Tamales (grain-free),
    245–48
  Pecan Brownies with Coconut Cajeta, 159–61,
    160
  Pecan Pie Empanadas, 167–68, *169*
  Tres Leches Cake with Coconut Whipped
    Cream, 172–75, *173*, *175*
Almond Flour Tortillas (Siete brand), 15
  Caldo de Res, 55
  Carne Guisada, 104, *105*
  Chilaquiles, 30, *31*
  Enchiladas de Res, *94*, 98–99
  Enchiladas Suizas, *94*, 100–101
  Flautas de Papa, 45–47, *46*
  Flautas Suaves, 70–71
  Huevos Rancheros, 32–33, *33*

  Mariachis, 21–23, *22*
  Migas, *18*, 19–20
  Tacos de Pescado (Fish Tacos), 64–66, *65*
  Tortilla Soup, *42*, 43–44
  Tostadas de Atún (Tuna Tostadas), 61–63, *62*
  Tostadas Siberias, *72*, 73–74
almond milk:
  Tres Leches Cake with Coconut Whipped
    Cream, 172–75, *173*, *175*
  Verde Sauce, 250–51
almond(s):
  Mazapan, *162*, 163
  Mole Almendrado, 107–8
ancho chiles, 7, *14*
appetizers:
  Fried Pickled Jalapeños and Carrots with Dairy-
    Free Ranch, 80, 81
  Shrimp Cocktail, 76, *77*
apple cider vinegar, 8
Apple Empanadas, *164*, 165–66
apricots, in Chamoy, *208*, 209
Arroz con Pollo, 120–21, *121*
Atole de Galleta, 194
avocado oil, 8
avocado(s):
  Dip, Creamy, 203
  Laredo-Style Sushi, *124*, 125–26

B

Barbacoa, 27–28, *29*
bean(s):
  black, in Mexican Chopped Salad, 148–49
  Charro, 140–41, *141*
  and Jalapeño Filling for Tamales, 245–46
  see also refried beans
beef:
  Barbacoa, 27–28, *29*
  Caldo de Res, 55
  Carne Asada Marinade for, 233
  Carne Asada Rub for, 232
  Carne Guisada, 104, *105*
  Enchiladas de Res, *94*, 98–99
  Filling for Tamales, 245–46
  Milanesa, 112, *113*
  Panchos, 240–41
  Picadillo, 118–19
  Pirata Tacos, *58*, 59–60
  Salpicón, 109–10, *111*
  Savory Empanadas, 252–53
black beans, in Mexican Chopped Salad, 148–49
Border-Town menu, *238*, 239–41
breakfast (desayuno), 17–39
  Aida's Breakfast menu, *226*, 227–28
  Apple Empanadas, *164*, 165–66
  Barbacoa, 27–28, *29*
  Café de Olla con Leche, 190, *191*
  Chicharrones en Salsa, 35
  Chilaquiles, 30, *31*
  Chocolate and Vanilla Conchas, *24*, 25–26
  Crispy Papas, *36*, 37
  Grain-Free Pancakes, 38, *39*
  Huevos a la Mexicana, 34
  Huevos Rancheros, 32–33, *33*
  Mariachis, 21–23, *22*
  Migas, *18*, 19–20
  Pecan Pie Empanadas, 167–68, *169*
  Salsa con Queso, Aida's, 228

Brownies, Pecan, with Coconut Cajeta, 159–61, *160*
Buñuelos, 254, *255*

C

cabbage:
  Caldo de Res, 55
  Slaw, 64
Café de Olla con Leche, 190, *191*
Cajeta, Coconut, *160*, 161
cakes:
  Tres Leches, with Coconut Whipped Cream, 172–75, *173*, *175*
calabacitas, in Calabaza con Pollo, 75
Calabaza con Pollo, 75
Caldo de Pollo, *52*, 53–54
Caldo de Res, 55
cantaloupe, in Fruit Cups, *88*, 89
caramel:
  Coconut Cajeta, *160*, 161
  Piloncillo, Flan with, 170, *171*
  Tres Leches Cake with Coconut Whipped Cream, 172–75, *173*, *175*
Carne Asada Marinade, 233
Carne Asada menu, *230*, 231–37, *234–35*
Carne Asada Rub, 232
Carne Guisada, 104, *105*
carrots:
  Arroz con Pollo, 120–21, *121*
  Escabeche, *214*, 215
  Fried Pickled Jalapeños and, with Dairy-Free Ranch, *80*, 81
  Grilled, with Mole and Crema, 144, *145*
cashew butter, in Almond Mazapan, *162*, 163
cashew crema, 8
Cashew Crema (recipes), 207
  Crispy Papas, *36*, 37
  for dairy-free crema, 90

Elotes Preparados, 86–87, *87*
Enchiladas Suizas, *94*, 100–101
Fried Chicken or Mushrooms, Grain-Free, 258–59, *259*
Jalapeño, 207
Papitas Preparadas, *84*, 85
Ranch Dipping Sauce, Dairy-Free, 81
Shrimp Tostadas, 68, *69*
Tostadas Siberias, *72*, 73–74
cashew milk:
    Flan with Caramel Piloncillo, 170, *171*
    Tres Leches Cake with Coconut Whipped Cream, 172–75, *173*, *175*
cashews, *13*
    Chipotle Mayo, 212
    Horchata, *179*, 182
cassava, 8
cassava flour, 8, *13*
    Apple Empanadas, *164*, 165–66
    Grain-Free Pancakes, 38, *39*
    Masa, Grain-Free, *218*, 219
    Masa Preparada for Tamales (grain-free), 245–48
    Pecan Pie Empanadas, 167–68, *169*
Cassava Flour Tortillas (Siete brand), 15
    Barbacoa, 27–28, *29*
    Enchiladas Verdes, *94*, 96–97
    Picadillo, 118–19
    Pirata Tacos, *58*, 59–60
    Shrimp Tostadas, 68, *69*
cauliflower:
    Rice, Mexican, 135
    Tacos de Coliflor, 114–15, *115*
Ceviche, Heart of Palm, 50, *51*
Chamoy, *208*, 209
    Fruit Cups, *88*, 89
Charro Beans, 140–41, *141*
cheese:
    cheddar, in Aida's Salsa con Queso, 228
    Cotija, Vegan, 86

Enchiladas de Res, *94*, 98–99
Enchiladas Suizas, *94*, 100–101
Frijolizzas, 122, *123*
Huevos Rancheros, 32–33, *33*
Laredo-Style Sushi, 125
Panchos, 240–41
Pirata Tacos, *58*, 59–60
Quesadillas, aka "Cheese Tacos," 116, *117*
Chia, Agua de Limón with, *179*, 183
chicharrones (fried pork rinds), 8
    en Salsa, 35
chicken:
    Arroz con Pollo, 120–21, *121*
    Calabaza con Pollo, 75
    Caldo de Pollo, *52*, 53–54
    Carne Asada Marinade for, 233
    Carne Asada Rub for, 232
    Enchiladas Suizas, *94*, 100–101
    Enchiladas Verdes, *94*, 96–97
    Flautas Suaves, 70–71
    Fried, Grain-Free, 258–59, *259*
    with Mole, *106*, 107–8
    Pozole, Red, 56–57, *57*
    Tortilla Soup, *42*, 43–44
    Tostadas Siberias, *72*, 73–74
Chickpea Flour Tortillas (Siete brand), 15
    Tacos de Pescado (Fish Tacos), 64–66, *65*
chickpeas:
    Chorizo, Vegan, 220–21, *221*
    Ground "Meat," Vegan, 222
Chilaquiles, 30, *31*
chile(s)/chile de arbol, 14
    Adobo, 220–21
    ancho, 7, *14*
    Chamoy, *208*, 209
    Chilaquiles, 30, *31*
    chipotle, 8
    Chipotle Mayo, 212
    dried, preparing before rehydrating, 220
    Escabeche, *214*, 215

chile(s) (*continued*)
  guajillo, 9, *14*
  habanero, 9, *14*
  Lime Seasoning, 210, *211*
  Oil, 199
  pasilla, *14*
  Salsa Tatemada, *200*, 201
  serrano, 12, *14*
  Toreados, 206
  see also jalapeño (chiles); poblano (chiles)
chipotle (chiles), 8
  Mayo, 212
chocolate:
  Hot, Mexican, *192*, 193
  Mole Almendrado, 107–8
  Pecan Brownies with Coconut Cajeta, 159–61,
    160
  and Vanilla Conchas, *24*, 25–26
Chopped Salad, Mexican, 148–49
Chorizo, Vegan, 220–21, *221*
Churros, Vegan, 156–58, *157*
cilantro, in Herby Pepita Parmesan (dairy-free),
    250
cinnamon, *13*
  Apple Empanadas, *164*, 165–66
  Atole de Galleta, 194
  Buñuelos, 254, *255*
  Café de Olla con Leche, 190, *191*
  Cashew Horchata, *179*, 182
  Chicken with Mole, *106*, 107–8
  Chocolate and Vanilla Conchas, *24*, 25–26
  Churros, Vegan, 156–58, *157*
  Mexican Hot Chocolate, *192*, 193
  Sugar, 156
cocktails:
  Mexican Martini, *186*, 187
  Paloma, 188, *189*
  Passion Fruit Margarita, 184, *185*
coconut aminos, 8
Coconut Cajeta, *160*, 161

Coconut Cream, Whipped, *173*, 174
coconut milk:
  Coconut Cajeta, *160*, 161
  Enchiladas Suizas, *94*, 100–101
  Flan with Caramel Piloncillo, 170, *171*
  Tres Leches Cake with Coconut Whipped
    Cream, 172–75, *173*, *175*
coconut oil, 8
coconut sugar, 9, *13*
coffee, in Café de Olla con Leche, 190, *191*
Cointreau, in Mexican Martini, *186*, 187
Conchas, Chocolate and Vanilla, *24*,
    25–26
condiments (*condimentos*), 197–215, *198*
  Carne Asada Marinade, 233
  Carne Asada Rub, 232
  Cashew Crema, 207
  Chamoy, *208*, 209
  Chile-Lime Seasoning, 210, *211*
  Chile Oil, 199
  Chiles Toreados, 206
  Chipotle Mayo, 212
  Creamy Avocado Dip, 203
  Escabeche, *214*, 215
  Jalapeño Crema, 207
  Marinated Red Onions, 213
  Salsa con Queso, Aida's, 228
  Salsa Cruda, 204, *205*
  Salsa de Aida, 202, *202*
  Salsa Tatemada, *200*, 201
corn:
  Caldo de Pollo, *52*, 53–54
  Caldo de Res, 55
  Elotes Preparados, 86–87, *87*
  Mexican Chopped Salad, 148–49
corn husks (in Tamales), 246
Cotija, Vegan (in Elotes Preparados), 86
Creamy Avocado Dip, 203
crema, dairy-free, 8
  see also Cashew Crema (recipes)

Crispy Papas, *36*, 37
Crispy Spiced Pepitas, 50

D

desserts (*postres*), 151–75
    Almond Mazapan, *162*, 163
    Apple Empanadas, *164*, 165–66
    Buñuelos, 254, *255*
    Churros, Vegan, 156–58, *157*
    Flan with Caramel Piloncillo, 170, *171*
    Mangonada Paletas, *152*, 154
    Pecan Brownies with Coconut Cajeta, 159–61, *160*
    Pecan Pie Empanadas, 167–68, *169*
    Tamarindo Paletas, *152*, 155
    Tres Leches Cake with Coconut Whipped
        Cream, 172–75, *173*, *175*
dinner (*cena*), 93–126
    Arroz con Pollo, 120–21, *121*
    Beef Milanesa, 112, *113*
    Beef Salpicón, 109–10, *111*
    Border-Town menu, *238*, 239–41
    Carne Asada menu, *230*, 231–37, *234–35*
    Carne Guisada, 104, *105*
    Chicken with Mole, *106*, 107–8
    Frijolizzas, 122, *123*
    Holidays menu, *242*, 243–54
    Laredo-Style Sushi, *124*, 125–26
    Picadillo, 118–19
    Quesadillas, aka "Cheese Tacos," 116, *117*
    Tacos de Coliflor (Cauliflower), 114–15, *115*
    see also enchiladas
dips:
    Avocado, Creamy, 203
    Ranch Dipping Sauce, Dairy-Free, 81
    Salsa con Queso, Aida's, 228
    Salsa Cruda, 204, *205*
    Salsa Tatemada, *200*, 201
drinks (*bebidas*), 177–94

    Agua de Limón with Chia, *179*, 183
    Agua Fresca de Jamaica (Iced Hibiscus Tea),
        178, *179*
    Atole de Galleta, 194
    Café de Olla con Leche, 190, *191*
    Cashew Horchata, *179*, 182
    Mexican Hot Chocolate, *192*, 193
    Mexican Martini, *186*, 187
    Paloma, 188, *189*
    Passion Fruit Margarita, 184, *185*
    Tamarind, Pineapple, and Ginger Agua Fresca,
        179, 181

E

eggs:
    Aida's Breakfast menu, *226*, 227–28
    Huevos a la Mexicana, 34
    Huevos Rancheros, 32–33, *33*
    Mariachis, 21–23, *22*
    Migas, *18*, 19–20
Elotes Preparados, 86–87, *87*
empanadas:
    Apple, *164*, 165–66
    Pecan Pie, 167–68, *169*
    Savory, 252–53
enchiladas, 95–101
    de Res, *94*, 98–99
    Suizas, *94*, 100–101
    Verdes, *94*, 96–97
Enchilada Sauce, 96, 98, 100
Escabeche, *214*, 215

F

Fajita
    Carne Asada Marinade for, 233
    Carne Asada menu, *230*, 231–37, *234–35*

Fajita (*continued*)
  Carne Asada Rub for, 232
  Fajita, Marinated, for Pirata Tacos, *58*, 59–60
  Panchos, 240–41
Fajita, Marinated, for Pirata Tacos, *58*, 59–60
fish and seafood:
  Shrimp Cocktail, 76, *77*
  Shrimp Tostadas, 68, *69*
  Tacos de Pescado (Fish Tacos), 64–66, *65*
  Tostadas de Atún (Tuna Tostadas), 61–63, *62*
Flan with Caramel Piloncillo, 170, *171*
flautas:
  de Papa, 45–47, *46*
  Suaves, 70–71
flours, *see* almond flour; cassava flour; white rice
  flour
Fresas con Crema, 90, *91*
fried (foods):
  Apple Empanadas, *164*, 165–66
  Beef Milanesa, 112, *113*
  Buñuelos, 254, *255*
  chicharrones, 8
  Chicharrones en Salsa, 35
  Chicken or Mushrooms, Grain-Free, 258–59,
    259
  Chilaquiles, 30, 31
  Churros, Vegan, 156–58, *157*
  Flautas de Papa, 45–47, *46*
  Migas, *18*, 19–20
  Pecan Pie Empanadas, 167–68, *169*
  Pickled Jalapeños and Carrots with Dairy-Free
    Ranch, *80*, 81
  Savory Empanadas, 252–53
  Shrimp Tostadas, 68, 69
  Tacos de Pescado (Fish Tacos), 64–66, *65*
  Tostadas de Atún (Tuna Tostadas), 61–63, *62*
Frijolizzas, 122, *123*
fruit:
  Agua Frescas de Jamaica (Iced Hibiscus Tea),
    178, *179*
  Apple Empanadas, *164*, 165–66
  Chamoy, *208*, 209
  Chile-Lime Seasoning, 210, *211*
  Cups, *88*, 89
  Fresas con Crema, 90, *91*
  Jicama, Mango, and Black Sesame Slaw, *146*,
    147
  Mexican Martini, *186*, 187
  Paletas, *152*, 154, 155
  Paloma, 188, *189*
  Passion Fruit Margarita, 184, *185*
  Tamarind, Pineapple, and Ginger Agua Fresca,
    179, 181
  Tres Leches Cake with Coconut Whipped
    Cream, 172–75, *173*, *175*
  see also specific fruits

G

ghee, 9
  Frijolizzas, 122, *123*
Ginger, Tamarind, and Pineapple Agua Fresca,
  179, 181
grapefruit juice, in Paloma, 188, *189*
grilled (foods):
  Alambres (Vegetable Skewers), 236–37
  Carne Asada menu, *230*, 231–37, *234–35*
  Carrots with Mole and Crema, 144, *145*
  Elotes Preparados, 86–87, *87*
  Nopalito Salad, 138–39
  Roasted Sweet Potatoes with Piloncillo and
    Butter, *142*, 143
  Salsa Tatemada, *200*, 201
  sweet potatoes, 143
Ground "Meat," Vegan, 222
  Enchiladas de Res, *94*, 98–99
  Savory Empanadas, 252–53
  Vegan Chorizo, 220–21, *221*
guajillo chiles, 9, *14*

Chamoy, *208*, 209
Chilaquiles, 30, *31*
Chile Oil, 199
Enchiladas de Res, *94*, 98–99
Red Pork or Chicken Pozole,
    56–57, *57*
Tamales, *244*, 245–49
Tortilla Soup, *42*, 43–44
Vegan Chorizo, 220–21, *221*

H

habanero chiles, 9, *14*
Heart of Palm Ceviche, 50, *51*
Herby Pepita Parmesan (dairy-free), 250
hibiscus flowers (jamaica), 9, *13*
    Agua Fresca de Jamaica (Iced Hibiscus Tea),
        178, *179*
    Chamoy, *208*, 209
Holidays menu, *242*, 243–54
hominy, in Red Pork or Chicken Pozole,
    56–57, *57*
Horchata, Cashew, *179*, 182
Hot Chocolate, Mexican, *192*, 193
Huevos a la Mexicana, 34
Huevos Rancheros, 32–33, *33*

jackfruit, in Vegan Shredded "Meat," 223
jalapeño (chiles), 9, *14*
    and Bean Filling for Tamales, 245–46
    Caldo de Pollo, *52*, 53–54
    Crema, 207
    Escabeche, *214*, 215
    Fried Pickled Carrots and, with Dairy-Free
        Ranch, *80*, 81
    Huevos a la Mexicana, 34
    Mexican Chopped Salad, 148–49
    Mexican Rice, 134
    Migas, *18*, 19–20

Nopalito Salad, 138–39
Picadillo, 118–19
pickled, in Salsa de Aida, 202, *202*
jamaica (hibiscus flowers), 9, *13*
    Agua Fresca de Jamaica (Iced Hibiscus Tea),
        178, *179*
Jicama, Mango, and Black Sesame Slaw,
    146, 147

L

Laredo-Style Sushi, *124*, 125–26
lime (juice), 9
    Agua de Limón with Chia, *179*,
        183
    Chile Seasoning, 210, *211*
    Mexican Martini, *186*, 187
    Paloma, 188, *189*
lunch (*almuerzo*), 41–76
    Calabaza con Pollo, 75
    Caldo de Pollo, *52*, 53–54
    Caldo de Res, 55
    Flautas de Papa, 45–47, *46*
    Flautas Suaves, 70–71
    Fried Chicken or Mushrooms, Grain-Free,
        258–59, *259*
    Heart of Palm Ceviche, 50, *51*
    Pirata Tacos, *58*, 59–60
    Red Pork or Chicken Pozole, 56–57, *57*
    Shrimp Cocktail, 76, *77*
    Shrimp Tostadas, 68, *69*
    Siete-Style Large Gathering menu, *256*,
        257–59
    Sopa de Fideo, 48, *49*
    Tacos de Pescado (Fish Tacos), 64–66,
        65
    Tortilla Soup, *42*, 43–44
    Tostadas de Atún (Tuna Tostadas), 61–63, *62*
    Tostadas Siberias, *72*, 73–74

M

Mangonada Paletas, *152*, 154
mango(s):
    Chamoy, *208*, 209
    Fruit Cups, *88*, 89
    Jicama, and Black Sesame Slaw, *146*, 147
    Mangonada Paletas, *152*, 154
    Raspas, 82, *83*
maple syrup, 9
    Agua Frescas de Jamaica (Iced Hibiscus Tea),
        178, *179*
    Apple Empanadas, *164*, 165–66
    Atole de Galleta, 194
    Cashew Horchata, *179*, 182
    Chamoy, *208*, 209
    Coconut Cajeta, *160*, 161
    Fresas con Crema, 90, *91*
    Ginger, Tamarind, and Pineapple Agua Fresca,
        179, 181
    Grain-Free Pancakes, 38, *39*
    Marinated Red Onions, 213
    Tamarindo Paletas, *152*, 155
    Tres Leches Cake with Coconut Whipped
        Cream, 172–75, *173*, *175*
Margarita, Passion Fruit, 184, *185*
Mariachis, 21–23, *22*
marinades:
    Carne Asada, 233
    Fajita, 59
Marinated Red Onions, 213
Martini, Mexican, *186*, 187
Masa, Grain-Free, *218*, 219
    Buñuelos made with, 254, *255*
    Masa Preparada for Tamales, made with, 245–48
    Savory Empanadas made with, 252–53
Mayo, Chipotle, 212
Mazapan, Almond, *162*, 163
"meat" (vegan alternatives):
    Chorizo, 220–21, *221*
    Ground, 222
    Shredded, 223
menus for gathering (*reuniones*), 225–59
    Aida's Breakfast, *226*, 227–28
    Border-Town, *238*, 239–41
    Carne Asada, *230*, 231–37, *234–35*
    Holidays, *242*, 243–54
    Siete-Style Large Gathering, *256*, 257–59
Mexican Cauliflower Rice, 135
Mexican Chopped Salad, 148–49
Mexican Hot Chocolate, *192*, 193
Mexican Martini, *186*, 187
Mexican oregano, 9, *13*
Mexican Rice, 134
    in Carne Asada menu, *230*, 231–37, *234–35*
Migas, *18*, 19–20
mole:
    Mole Almendrado, 107–8
    Chicken with Mole Almendrado, *106*, 107–8
    Grilled Carrots with Crema and, 144, *145*
mushrooms:
    Alambres (Vegetable Skewers), 236–37
    Chicken Fried, Grain-Free, 259
    Chorizo, Vegan, 220–21, *221*
    Ground "Meat," Vegan, 222
    portobello, in Pirata Tacos, *58*, 59–60

N

Nopalito Salad, 138–39

O

olives, in Elotes Preparados, 86–87, *87*
olive brine, in Mexican Martini, *186*, 187
onions:
    Alambres (Vegetable Skewers), 236–37
    Escabeche, *214*, 215

Red, Marinated, 213
Salsa Tatemada, *200*, 201
options (*opciones*), 217–23
    Chorizo, Vegan, 220–21, *221*
    Cotija, Vegan, 86
    Ground "Meat," Vegan, 222
    Masa, Grain-Free, *218*, 219
    Shredded "Meat," Vegan, 223
orange juice:
    Agua Fresca de Jamaica (Iced Hibiscus Tea),
        178, *179*
    Carne Asada Marinade, 233
    Heart of Palm Ceviche, 50, *51*
    Mangonada Paletas, *152*, 154
    Mexican Martini, *186*, 187
    Vegan Shredded "Meat," 223
oregano, Mexican, 9, *13*

P

paletas (popsicles), 153–55
    Mangonada, *152*, 154
    Tamarindo, *152*, 155
Paloma, 188, *189*
    in Siete-Style Large Gathering menu, *256*,
        257–59
Pancakes, Grain-Free, 38, *39*
    in Aida's Breakfast menu, *226*, 227–28
Panchos, 240–41
    in Border-Town menu, *238*, 239–41
Papas, Crispy, *36*, 37
    in Aida's Breakfast menu, *226*,
        227–28
Papitas Preparadas, *84*, 85
    in Border-Town menu, *238*, 239–41
pasilla chiles, *14*
    Chamoy, *208*, 209
Passion Fruit Margarita, 184, *185*
    Carne Asada menu, *230*, 231–37, *234–35*

pecan(s):
    Brownies with Coconut Cajeta, 159–61, *160*
    Chorizo, Vegan, 220–21, *221*
    Ground "Meat," Vegan, 222
    Pie Empanadas, 167–68, *169*
    Savory Empanadas, 252–53
pepita(s) (pumpkin seeds):
    Chile Oil, 199
    Crispy Spiced, 50
    Heart of Palm Ceviche with Crispy Spiced, 50
    Parmesan, Herby (dairy-free), 250
peppers (bell):
    Alambres (Vegetable Skewers), 236–37
    Mexican Chopped Salad, 148–49
    Refried Beans (recipe), *130*, 131–32
Picadillo, 118–19
pickled (foods):
    Escabeche, *214*, 215
    Jalapeños and Carrots, Fried, with Dairy-Free
        Ranch, *80*, 81
    Marinated Red Onions, 213
piloncillo (Mexican brown sugar), 12, *13*
    Café de Olla con Leche, 190, *191*
    Caramel, Flan with, 170, *171*
    Roasted Sweet Potatoes with Butter and, *142*, 143
pineapple:
    Fruit Cups, *88*, 89
    Tamarind, and Ginger Agua Fresca, *179*, 181
Pirata Tacos, *58*, 59–60
    in Border-Town menu, *238*, 239–41
pizza sauce, in Frijolizzas, 122, *123*
poblano (chiles), 12, *14*
    Alambres (Vegetable Skewers), 236–37
    Rice (*arroz verde*, or green rice), 136–37
    Verde Sauce, 250–51
popsicles, *see* paletas
pork:
    Pozole, Red, 56–57, *57*
    Red Pork or Chicken Pozole, 56–57, *57*
    rinds, fried, in Chicharrones en Salsa, 35

portobello mushrooms, in Pirata Tacos, *58*, 59–60

potato(es):
Caldo de Pollo, *52*, 53–54
Caldo de Res, 55
Carne Guisada, 104, *105*
chips, in Laredo-Style Sushi, *124*, 125–26
chips, in Papitas Preparadas, *84*, 85
Crispy Papas, *36*, 37
Flautas de Papa, 45–47, *46*
Mariachis, 21–23, *22*
Picadillo, 118–19
Savory Empanadas, 252–53
see sweet potatoes

potato starch:
Chocolate and Vanilla Conchas, *24*, 25–26
Tres Leches Cake with Coconut Whipped
    Cream, 172–75, *173*, *175*

Pozole, Red Pork or Chicken, 56–57, *57*
in Holidays menu, *242*, 243–54

prunes, in Chamoy, *208*, 209

pumpkin seeds:
Crispy Spiced Pepitas, 50
Herby Pepita Parmesan (dairy-free), 250

Q

Quesadillas, aka "Cheese Tacos," 116, *117*

R

Ranch Dipping Sauce, Dairy-Free, 81
Ranchero Sauce, 32
Raspas, Mango, 82, *83*
Red Pork or Chicken Pozole, 56–57, *57*
in Holidays menu, *242*, 243–54
refried bean(s):
in Aida's Breakfast menu, *226*, 227–28
in Border-Town menu, *238*, 239–41

Carne Asada menu, *230*, 231–37, *234–35*
Frijolizzas, 122, *123*
Huevos Rancheros, 32–33, *33*
and Jalapeño Filling for Tamales, 245–46
Panchos, 240–41
Pirata Tacos, *58*, 59–60

Refried Beans (recipe), *130*, 131–32

rice:
Arroz con Pollo, 120–21, *121*
Cauliflower, Mexican, 135
Laredo-Style Sushi, *124*, 125–26
Mexican, 134
Poblano (*arroz verde*, or green rice), 136–37

rice flour, *see* white rice flour
rolls, in Frijolizzas, 122, *123*
Rub, Carne Asada, 232

S

salads:
Cabbage Slaw, 64
Chopped, Mexican, 148–49
Jicama, Mango, and Black Sesame Slaw, *146*,
    147
Nopalito, 138–39

Salsa con Queso, Aida's, 228
in Aida's Breakfast menu, *226*, 227–28
Salsa Cruda, 204, *205*
Carne Asada menu, *230*, 231–37, *234–35*
Salsa de Aida, 202, *202*
in Aida's Breakfast menu, *226*, 227–28
Salsa Roja in Flautas de Papa, 45
Salsa Tatemada, *200*, 201
Salsa Verde in Chicharrones en Salsa, 35, 70–71

sauces:
Adobo, 220–21
Cocktail, 76
Enchilada (green), 96, 100
Enchilada (red), 98

Mole Almendrado, 107–8
Ranch Dipping, Dairy-Free, 81
Ranchero, 32
Salsa con Queso, Aida's, 228
Verde, 250–51
sausage:
Charro Beans, 140–41, *141*
Chorizo, Vegan, 220–21, *221*
Savory Empanadas, 252–53
in Holidays menu, *242*, 243–54
scallions:
Crispy Papas, *36*, 37
Salsa Tatemada, *200*, 201
Tostadas de Atún (Tuna Tostadas), 61–63, *62*
Seasoning, Chile-Lime, 210, *211*
serrano chiles, 12, *14*
Chiles Toreados, 206
shortbread cookies:
Atole de Galleta, 194
Fresas con Crema, 90, *91*
Shredded "Meat," Vegan, 223
shrimp:
Cocktail, 76, *77*
Laredo-Style Sushi, *124*, 125–26
Tostadas, 68, *69*
sides (*guarniciónes*), 129–49
Charro Beans, 140–41, *141*
Escabeche, *214*, 215
Grilled Carrots with Mole and Crema, 144, *145*
Jicama, Mango, and Black Sesame Slaw, *146*, 147
Mexican Cauliflower Rice, 135
Mexican Chopped Salad, 148–49
Mexican Rice, 134
Nopalito Salad, 138–39
Poblano Rice (*arroz verde*, or green rice), 136–37
Refried Beans, *130*, 131–32
Roasted Sweet Potatoes with Piloncillo and Butter, *142*, 143

Siete-Style Large Gathering menu, *256*, 257–59
slaws:
Cabbage, 64
Jicama, Mango, and Black Sesame, *146*, 147
snacks (*botanas*), 79–90
Chamoy for, *208*, 209
Elotes Preparados, 86–87, *87*
Escabeche, *214*, 215
Fresas con Crema, 90, *91*
Fried Pickled Jalapeños and Carrots with Dairy-Free Ranch, *80*, 81
Fruit Cups, *88*, 89
Mango Raspas, 82, *83*
Papitas Preparadas, *84*, 85
see also sweet treats
Sopa de Fideo, 48, *49*
soups:
Caldo de Pollo, *52*, 53–54
Caldo de Res, 55
Red Pork or Chicken Pozole, 56–57, *57*
Sopa de Fideo, 48, *49*
Tortilla, *42*, 43–44
spaghetti:
Sopa de Fideo, 48, *49*
Verde (Green Spaghetti), *242*, 250–51
strawberries:
Fresas con Crema, 90, *91*
Tres Leches Cake with Coconut Whipped Cream, 172–75, *173*, *175*
sugar:
Cinnamon (recipe) in Vegan Churros, 156
coconut, 9, *13*
see also piloncillo; sweet treats
Sushi, Laredo-Style, *124*, 125–26
sweet potatoes:
Roasted, with Piloncillo and Butter, *142*, 143
roasting on grill, 143
sweet treats:
Almond Mazapan, *162*, 163
Apple Empanadas, *164*, 165–66

sweet treats (*continued*)

Buñuelos, 254, *255*

Chocolate and Vanilla Conchas, *24*, 25–26

Churros, Vegan, 156–58, *157*

Flan with Caramel Piloncillo, 170, *171*

Fresas con Crema, 90, *91*

Mangonada Paletas, *152*, 154

Mango Raspas, 82, *83*

Mexican Hot Chocolate, *192*, 193

Pecan Brownies with Coconut Cajeta, 159–61, *160*

Pecan Pie Empanadas, 167–68, *169*

Tamarindo Paletas, *152*, 155

Tres Leches Cake with Coconut Whipped Cream, 172–75, *173*

T

tacos:

de Coliflor (Cauliflower), 114–15, *115*

de Pescado (Fish Tacos), 64–66, *65*

Mariachis, 21–23, *22*

Pirata, *58*, 59–60

Quesadillas, aka "Cheese Tacos," 116, *117*

Tamales, *244*, 245–49

assembling, *247*, 248

Bean and Jalapeño Filling for, 245–46

in Holidays menu, *242*, 243–54

Beef Filling for, 245–46

Masa Preparada for, 245–48

steaming, 248–49

tamarind, 12, *13*

Chamoy, *208*, 209

Paletas, *152*, 155

Pineapple, and Ginger Agua Fresca, *179*, 181

tequila blanco:

Mexican Martini, *186*, 187

Paloma, 188, *189*

Passion Fruit Margarita, 184, *185*

tomatillos:

Chicharrones en Salsa, 35

Enchilada Suizas, 96, 100

Enchiladas Verdes, *94*, 96–97

Flautas Suaves, 70–71

Mexican Chopped Salad, 148–49

Salsa Verde, 70–71

tomato(es):

Calabaza con Pollo, 75

Caldo de Pollo, *52*, 53–54

Carne Guisada, 104, *105*

Charro Beans, 140–41, *141*

cherry, in Alambres (Vegetable Skewers), 236–37

Chilaquiles, 30, *31*

Enchilada Sauce, 98

Heart of Palm Ceviche, 50, *51*

Huevos a la Mexicana, 34

Mexican Cauliflower Rice, 135

Mexican Rice, 134

Migas, *18*, 19–20

Mole Almendrado, 107–8

Nopalito Salad, 138–39

Picadillo, 118–19

Ranchero Sauce, 32

Salsa con Queso, Aida's, 228

Salsa Cruda, 204, *205*

Salsa de Aida, 202, *202*

Salsa Roja, 45

Salsa Tatemada, *200*, 201

Shrimp Cocktail, 76, *77*

Sopa de Fideo, 48, *49*

Tortilla Soup, *42*, 43–44

tortillas, Siete brand:

Almond Flour, 15. *See also recipes under* Almond Flour Tortillas

Cassava Flour, 15.. *See also recipes under* Cassava Flour Tortillas

Chickpea Flour, 15
  Tacos de Pescado (Fish Tacos), 64–66, *65*
tortilla(s):
  Chilaquiles, 30, *31*
  chips, in Panchos, 240–41
  Flautas de Papa, 45–47, *46*
  Flautas Suaves, 70–71
  Huevos Rancheros, 32–33, *33*
  Migas, *18*, 19–20
  Quesadillas, aka "Cheese Tacos," 116, *117*
  Soup, *42*, 43–44
  see also enchiladas; tacos; tostadas
tostadas:
  de Atún (Tuna Tostadas), 61–63, *62*
  Beef Salpicón, 109–10, *111*
  Shrimp, 68, *69*
  Siberias, *72*, 73–74
Tres Leches Cake with Coconut Whipped Cream, 172–75, *173*, *175*
Tuna Tostadas (Tostadas de Atún), 61–63, *62*

V

vegan:
  Chorizo, 220–21, *221*
  Churros, 156–58, *157*
  Cotija, 86
  Ground "Meat," 222

Shredded "Meat," 223
vegetables:
  Alambres (Vegetable Skewers), 236–37
  Calabaza con Pollo, 75
  Caldo de Pollo, *52*, 53–54
  Caldo de Res, 55
  Carne Asada Marinade for, 233
  Carne Asada Rub for, 232
  Tacos de Coliflor (Cauliflower), 114–15, *115*
  See specific vegetables
Verde Sauce in Spaghetti Verde, 250–51

W

watermelon, in Fruit Cups, *88*, 89
whipped cream:
  Coconut, *173*, 174
  Fresas con Crema, 90, *91*
white rice flour:
  Chocolate and Vanilla Conchas, *24*, 25–26
  Churros, Vegan, 156–58, *157*

Z

zucchini:
  Alambres (Vegetable Skewers), 236–37
  Calabaza con Pollo, 75
  Caldo de Pollo, *52*, 53–54
  Caldo de Res, 55

ABOUT THE AUTHORS

THE GARZAS are a third-generation Mexican-American family from Laredo, Texas. The seven (Siete!) members of the Garza family—Aida, Bobby, Linda, Roberto, Veronica, Becky, and Miguel—make up the original siete, whose collective journey to health paved the way for what is now Siete Family Foods. The Garzas' values and traditions of family, love, and doing everything together (Juntos es Mejor!) are what shapes the company culture at Siete, and are at the heart of everything they do.